W9-CAM-335

THE BEST OF
Disney

THE BEST OF

Disney

NEIL SINYARD

Twin Books

Portland House
A Division of Crown Publishers, Inc.

This 1988 edition published by
Portland House, distributed by
Crown Publishers, Inc.
225 Park Avenue South
New York, NY 10003

Produced by
Twin Books Corp.
15 Sherwood Place
Greenwich, CT 06830
USA

Printed in Hong Kong

Library of Congress Cataloging-in-Publication Data
Sinyard, Neil.
   The best of Disney.
   1. Disney, Walt, 1901-1966—Criticism and interpretation.   2. Walt
Disney Productions.   3. Animated films—United States—History and
criticism. [1. Disney, Walt, 1901-1966—Criticism and
interpretation.   2. Walt Disney Productions.   3. Animated films—
History and criticism]   I. Title.
PN1998.3.D57S56   1988'   791.43'092'4   87-36614

ISBN 0-517-65346-X

h g f e d c b a

PAGE 1: Walt Disney with Mickey and Donald, 1956.
PAGES 2-3: *The Reluctant Dragon*.
PAGES 4-5: The evolution of Mickey Mouse.

Contents

Introduction

When you wish upon a star your dreams come true – if you happen to have the unique industriousness and vision of a Walt Disney. From modest beginnings he was to grow into the undisputed emperor of twentieth century mass entertainment.

Disney's career is one of the most innovative in the history of the cinema. Unfortunately one of the problems of being a household name is that you can be taken for granted. Disney's achievement has sometimes been dismissed as merely the ability to package and export American cuteness and sentimentality. The movies certainly reflect the simple convictions of the man, but there is nothing simple about the staggering technique of the best of Disney's animated films. Uncle Walt might have inspired the love of children, but he also had the unstinting admiration of fellow professionals like Alfred Hitchcock, Frank Capra, Sergei Eisenstein and, recently and most noticeably, Steven Spielberg. He had the respect of a modern master like Henri Matisse, cartoonist David Low thought Disney the 'most significant figure in graphic arts since Leonardo,' and the American cartoonist and critic Don Herrold considered the artistry of Disney to rank higher than that of Rembrandt.

Disney did not do the animation himself, of course, and in

LEFT: Me and my shadow. Walt Disney and his alter ego, Mickey Mouse.

ABOVE RIGHT: Walt Disney at the age of ten months.

RIGHT: Walt Disney's birthplace: 1249 Tripp Avenue, Chicago.

selecting the best films from different periods of his career this book has taken some care to give appropriate credit to the many fine animators who worked with him. Yet they would be the first to acknowledge that it was Disney who ran the show. To use a musical analogy, Disney might not have composed the score, but he supervised its composition, orchestrated it and conducted it. And if at the end he took the lion's share of the credit, this also involved taking the full force of the criticism when it came.

Walt Disney was born in Chicago on 5 December 1901, one of a family of four boys and a girl. The family soon moved to a farm in Marceline, Missouri and then in 1910 went to live in Kansas City. Of his early life Disney seems to have remembered with particular affection his period on the farm – the rural values of many of his movies probably stem from that time. Of the members of his family, two played a significant role in Disney's life: his father Elias, whom Disney described as 'a failure at everything' (ineffectual fathers crop up a lot in

his films) and whose failure seems to have made Disney ever more determined to excel himself; and his elder brother, Roy, who was to follow Walt into the film industry and become his business manager, his best friend, and ultimately president of Walt Disney Productions.

Disney studied art and photography in high school and also served for a year as an ambulance driver in France at the end of the First World War. (A photograph of him at this time by the side of his ambulance has an intriguing cartoon drawing visible on his vehicle – perhaps a sign of things to come.) On his return from France he obtained employment as a commercial artist in Kansas City, working for a film company that made animated commercials for showing in city cinemas. Disney began to branch out with his own full-blown cartoons, mainly on fairy-tale themes such as Cinderella, Puss in Boots, Red Riding Hood, and Jack and the Beanstalk. He was partnered by a brilliant young artist, Ub Iwerks. When Disney set up a base for production of these

ABOVE: The Kansas City Film Ad company, where Disney had his first job after returning from Europe. Walt is sitting on the brick post on the right; Ub Iwerks is standing seventh from the right.

LEFT: Walt stands beside the ambulance he drove in France during World War I. Notice the cartoon on his vehicle.

RIGHT: Walt hard at work on one of his first 'Laugh-O-Grams,' on the theme of Jack and the Beanstalk, in 1922.

cartoons in California he sent for Iwerks to join him from Kansas City, Missouri. Aside from the 1930s when he went freelance in order to do two of his own cartoon series, *Flip the Frog* and *Willie Whopper*, Iwerks worked for the Disney organization until his death in 1971. During this time he succeeded in conceiving and perfecting many discoveries in animation and special effects.

Disney launched a series called *Alice Comedies* which was a combination of primitive cartoon and equally rudimentary live-action, and then moved on to a new series called *Oswald the Lucky Rabbit*. When his distributor (who owned the rights) not only took the character of Oswald away from him but also enticed away some of his animators, Disney resolved never again to relinquish ownership of his films. As it happened he had a better idea brewing. Was there, Walt Disney wondered, material here for a potential series – was there a future in the idea of a cartoon mouse?

ABOVE: Walt Disney's letterhead.

LEFT: Disney and a multitude of Mickeys.

RIGHT: A rare shot of Disney behind the camera.

The Mousetro
Animated Cartoons 1928-1937

When the lights dimmed again I started to close my eyes, but as the picture flashed on the screen I opened them wide as saucers . . . A bright, perky mouse – with a saucy, squeaky voice – was burlesquing a piano recital, banging on the piano with his hands, his feet, his nose, even with his tail. And picture and sound were beautifully synchronized. The tired crew howled with laughter. This was new and wonderful entertainment.

This is director Frank Capra's account in his autobiography, *The Name Above The Title*, of his first glimpse of Mickey Mouse. If the sight had this impact on a hardened professional like Capra, one can imagine the effect Mickey was to have on the general public. The decade following the introduction of Mickey Mouse is one of the great periods of Disney cartoon-making when the standards of animation were to rise considerably. For Disney not only introduced Mickey to the film cartoon; he introduced characters like Pluto, Goofy and Donald Duck and innovations like the Silly Symphonies; and he was to break new ground in his experiments with sound and color. It was during this period that Disney established and consolidated his pre-eminence in the field of the cartoon, surrounding himself with a team of top animators, many of whom were to remain with the Disney organization for the next forty years.

What was Disney's secret? Was it his method of preparation – the elaborate storyboard of every short so that each animator knew exactly how the story was meant to go and could contribute and embellish ideas within this clear structure? Was it his method of training? Disney animators were known to attend Don Graham's art classes for lessons in drawing and anatomy and even psychology. Or was it simply that he paid more? An employee's name might not appear in the list of the credits for a Disney short, but there were other rewards – a $5 bonus for a gag used in a cartoon, a $100 bonus if an idea led to a complete cartoon, and for a top animator

LEFT: Mickey at the height of his popularity: from *Mickey's Gala Premiere* (1933).

ABOVE RIGHT: The poster for *Father Noah's Ark* (1933), a sprightly Silly Symphony with one of Disney's merriest menageries.

RIGHT: Mickey's supporting cast in the process of becoming stars: from *Donald and Pluto* (1936).

LEFT: Goofy's debut: he is the one wearing the hat in this crowd scene from *Mickey's Revue* (1932).

ABOVE RIGHT: Mickey heads for a fall in *Mickey Steps Out* (1931); as usual, Pluto is no help.

ABOVE FAR RIGHT: Mickey, with friends, in typical musical mood: from *Mickey's Follies* (1929).

BELOW RIGHT: Mickey tames and entertains Pluto in these publicity drawings for *The Mad Dog* (1932).

like Art Babbitt, a lifestyle that during the Depression could consist of a large house, two servants and three cars.

All this no doubt contributed to excellent work, but there was a lot more besides, and much of it had to do with Disney's own perception and perfectionism. He might have the power to go out and hire 300 artists, many of them from art school, as he did in 1935, but just as many were drawn to Disney studios themselves by the sheer quality of the work. For Art Babbitt the crucial film was *The Skeleton Dance* (1929), which knocked all ideas out of his head of becoming a psychiatrist and persuaded him to become an animator instead. For another top Disney artist, Ward Kimball, the turning point was *Father Noah's Ark* (1933) – shortly afterward he quit his job, talked his mother into giving him a lift to Los Angeles, and arrived at the studio gate with a portfolio of his work and a request for employment.

Not everyone who worked with Disney liked the man for he could be aloof and quick-tempered, but everyone without exception respected and admired his judgment and zeal, and his ability to bring out the best in people. He knew what worked with audiences. He had a fantastic story sense and an instinct for the elements of film comedy, such as slapstick and double-takes, that rivaled Mack Sennett's outstanding abilities. Above all he had a very clear idea in his mind of what made a good animator. He once spelled out the qualities he looked for: good draughtsmanship, of course; an ability to vizualize action; a feeling for comic caricature ('to take a natural human action,' as Disney put it, 'and see the exaggerated funny side of it'); an ability to imagine what takes place in the minds of an audience; and most importantly, an ability to enter into the character of the animated figure. Animation is both movement *and* expression, Disney thought. It involves not only the ability to draw but the ability to *act*.

It is for this reason that Disney asked his story department head, Ted Sears, to draw up a detailed analysis of the key Disney characters, so that any animator entrusted to draw one of them could refer to these portraits to ensure his drawing remained in keeping with the character. Mickey Mouse 'is not a clown . . .' noted Sears. 'He is neither silly nor dumb. His comedy depends entirely on the situation he is placed in. He is most amusing when in a serious predicament trying to accomplish some purpose under difficulties . . .' *The Band Concert* (1935) is a definitive example of that. Pluto's character 'should always be that of a real dog . . . His feelings are easily hurt when scolded; he is foolhardy rather than brave.' Cartoons such as *Playful Pluto* (1934) where he gets stuck to a piece of flypaper, or *Pluto's Judgment Day* (1935) where the sensitive animal endures trial by monstrous cats, superbly exemplify his character. Fred Moore directed the animation of Mickey, and Norman Ferguson of Pluto. Goofy, according to animator Art Babbitt, 'was the kind of person who always thinks long and carefully before doing anything – and then does it wrong.' Goofy had made his first appearance in *Mickey's Revue* (1932), and a definitive example of his oafishness would be found in the classic cartoon *Moving Day* (1936).

The creation that made Disney most famous was Mickey Mouse. The story goes that Disney had dreamed up the legendary mouse while traveling on a train taking him from New York to Los Angeles. It was his wife, Lillian, who had christened the mouse Mickey. It was Disney's partner, Ub Iwerks, who first drew Mickey's unmistakable features, basically constructing them around two large circles for the head and the body (circles were the easiest shape to animate effectively), two smaller circles for the ears, arms and legs like hosepipes, plump hands, large feet, short pants and a

nose like a small plum. Disney did not draw Mickey very well, but he provided the voice of Mickey for the next twenty years and, in a sense, became Mickey's adopted father.

Mickey Mouse has been likened to Chaplin's tramp and described, by Graham Greene, as a rodent Fred Astaire, but Disney always saw him as a character not unlike himself – a nice fellow, harmless, ordinary, always getting into scrapes but in the end always coming up smiling. Mickey's phenomenal popularity made him something of a problem child for Disney, because parents demanded that he should not drink, smoke or do anything that might set a bad example for youth.

In order to get round that Disney came up with several different solutions. Firstly he rang the changes not through developments in Mickey's character but through putting him in a bewildering range of occupations or roles, from gaucho to Gulliver, cowboy to carpenter, tailor to teamster. Also he brought in other characters, so Mickey's role was often a supporting one. He has to rescue Pluto from the title character of *The Mad Doctor* (1933), an ingenious parody of the 1931 horror classic *Frankenstein*; and he costars with Donald Duck and Goofy in *Lonesome Ghosts* (1937). His star quality still shone through in inspired projects like *Thru the Mirror*

LEFT: Mickey and Donald are threatened with eviction in *Moving Day* (1936), one of the best of the 1930s' cartoons. Goofy produced some inspired clowning, Mickey was at his most defiantly dignified, and Donald, as always, kept on tying himself up in his own tirades.

RIGHT: Misplaced confidence: the haughty hare prepares for what he thinks will be an easy victory in *The Tortoise and the Hare* (1935).

BELOW: *Who Killed Cock Robin?* (1935) was a Silly Symphony that became controversial because of its alleged violence. Jenny Wren, whom Robin loves, is drawn as a comic caricature of Mae West.

(1936), a sort of Mickey in Wonderland, and in his performance in *Fantasia* (1940) of the sorcerer's apprentice. However, Mickey's early prankishness was now being transferred to a new character who began to rival Mickey in popularity – his name was Donald Duck.

Unusually, Disney had gotten the idea for this character not from a drawing but from a voice. He had heard Clarence Nash on the radio reciting 'Mary had a little lamb' in a duck's voice and had recognized the potential for a cartoon character. Donald made his debut in a supporting role in *The Wise Little Hen* (1934) but came into his own in *Orphans' Benefit* (1934), a cartoon in which he becomes enraged by the behavior of the child audience – Donald rarely got on with children. In *Donald's Nephews* (1938), a satire both on parental handbooks and on the Dead End Kids ('after all, little children are only angels without wings'), his life is made a misery by Huey, Dewey and Louie. The essence of Donald Duck was his aggression. 'An ego show-off,' was animator Dick Lundy's description of the character, 'he can dish it out but he can't take it.' Curiously he was popular because he had precisely those qualities of anger and abrasiveness that people seek to repress. 'I do love him so,' says the heroine of Donald Duck in David Lean's *Brief Encounter* (1945), 'his dreadful energy, his blind, frustrated rages . . .'

In addition to the memorable cartoon characters created, Disney's contribution to animation in the 1930s should be recognized through his marvelous series of Silly Symphony cartoons which provided an opportunity to be more adventurous in style, theme and tone. The idea for the series came from Disney's musical director of the time, Carl Stalling, who subsequently left Disney to become music director for Warner Brothers' Looney Tunes. As the title indicates,

music often played an important role in this series, as in *Music Land* (1935) which is a kind of contest between jazz and classical music. There were also hilarious impressions – of drunkenness in *The Country Cousin* (1936) and even of Hollywood in *Mother Goose Goes Hollywood* (1938) which draws Greta Garbo as an aloof Margery Daw and Katharine Hepburn as a very plaintive Little Bo Peep ('I've lost my sheep, I can't find it anywhere, really I can't'). This tone of mischief sometimes led to outright mayhem, and there were even complaints about the violence of *Who Killed Cock Robin?* (1935) – significantly Alfred Hitchcock uses it as counterpoint to a tense scene that takes place in a cinema in his thriller *Sabotage* (1936).

Some commentators have suggested that toward the middle of the 1930s Disney's cartoons were becoming less fantasized and more didactic and idealistic. *The Flying Mouse* (1934) offers a moral homily on the theme of 'be yourself'; *The Tortoise and the Hare* (1935) is a cautionary tale of premature arrogance; *Grasshopper and the Ants* (1934) punctures the philosophy of 'the world owes me a living.' The truth is that by this time Disney was probably looking for bigger mountains to climb – notably the feature-length animated film. Although he continued to produce splendid cartoon shorts, Disney's energies expanded into other areas after the mid-1930s, and his great period was over by the end of the decade. But what a legacy of material, and what pleasure it brought to a Depression-stricken America! It makes one understand that definition of 'Americanism' that appeared in *The Saturday Evening Post* (21 May 1938): 'spending millions of dollars to make spectacular movies; sticking through them to see Mickey Mouse.' Small wonder that Walt Disney was known in the movie industry simply as 'The Mousetro.'

Steamboat Willie
1928

Steamboat Willie is significant as the cartoon which made Mickey Mouse a star. Strictly speaking it was not Mickey's debut. He had already appeared in *Plane Crazy* (1928) as a sort of rodent Lindbergh, and in *Gallopin' Gaucho* (1928), but these were not released until after *Steamboat Willie*. The character was not at that time quite fully formed. Although he was sporting more clothes than in the first two cartoons, he had not yet acquired all his trademarks – in *Steamboat* he wears shoes but not his famous white gloves. Yet the impact of the film when premiered at the Colony Theater in New York on 18 November 1928 was tremendous, for the cartoon had not one, but two, unique features – Mickey and sound.

After the enormous success of *The Jazz Singer* (1927) which introduced sound into motion pictures, Disney had been determined to make the first sound cartoon. What he wanted was a complete synchronization between sound and image, but how could this be achieved? With the assistance of his musical arranger Carl Stalling, his chief animating partner Ub Iwerks, and a new recruit to the Disney organization, Wilfred Jackson, Disney sought to solve the problem.

'Walt told us he knew how fast the film is going to go: 90 feet a minute, or 24 frames per second,' recalled Wilfred Jackson many years later. 'But he couldn't see any way to tell how fast the music would go. Now, I knew what a metronome was, so I brought one to work and showed it to Walt. I set the metronome at 60 and it ticked sixty times in a minute – one tick every twenty-four frames. I set it at 120 and got a tick every twelve frames. I could make it tick in any multiple of frames Walt wanted. Then I got out my harmonica and played "Turkey in the Straw" while the metronome ticked away, and Walt could tell how fast the music was going.' From this basis, it became possible to time the action to the rhythm of the music. The first recording session for *Steamboat Willie* was a disaster, because the conductor failed to appreciate the importance of following to the letter the precise tempo markings, but once that was grasped, soundtrack and cartoon action fitted as snugly as a Mickey glove.

Indeed, to this day the technique of precise co-ordination of musical soundtrack to the movement on the screen is called, in movie slang, 'Mickey Mousing.'

There was a famous occasion during the experiment when the Disneys and their collaborators presented a short sequence of *Steamboat Willie* with improvised, primitive soundtrack to their wives and girlfriends. To cut down on projection noise Roy Disney ran the film through the projector from outside the window of the house, while inside Walt, Iwerks and others performed their impromptu sound accompaniment of tinpans, whistles, cowbells and washboard to the beat of a metronome. Its impact in these domestic surroundings was somewhat muted, by all accounts, but the historical importance of the movie was soon recognized in more orthodox film contexts. As the film historian Alexander Walker pointed out in his book about the cinema's tortuous transition to sound, *The Shattered Silents*, *Steamboat Willie* had 'the most imaginative use of sound to be heard on the screen at that date – and for a long time to come.'

The plot is relatively conventional: Mickey rescues Minnie from the unwelcome attentions of Pete. However, the highlight of the film is a musical interlude, which could almost be

ABOVE: Mickey in *Steamboat Willie* (1928). He has not yet acquired his characteristic white gloves.

LEFT: Mickey and Minnie in *Plane Crazy* (1928), with Mickey as a cartoon Lindbergh. *Plane Crazy* was made before *Steamboat Willie* but released afterward.

ABOVE RIGHT: The soundtrack comes into its own in *Steamboat Willie* as Mickey transforms livestock into a live orchestra.

RIGHT: Ub Iwerks drawing Mickey Mouse. He could always draw Mickey better than Disney could.

FAR RIGHT: Dancing on their own graves: the skeletons enjoy a night out in *The Skeleton Dance* (1929).

subtitled 'Animal Fun,' when the boat's cargo of animals is transformed into the instruments of an orchestra. A goat nibbles the sheet music of 'Turkey in the Straw,' but when its tail is cranked up like a starting handle the notes fly out of its mouth in the form of a melody. A sow is squeezed like a bagpipe; a cow's teeth are tapped in the manner of a xylophone; and we hear the sound of music in the squeal of pigs and the wail of cats. It is a marvelous example of the surreal imagination of early Disney and what came to be called 'Cinesymphony,' the marriage of music and animation that was to culminate most spectacularly in *Fantasia* (1940).

The Skeleton Dance
1929

The Skeleton Dance is one of the most brilliant of Disney's early shorts. It so 'floored' (his own word) the young animator Art Babbitt when he saw it that he resolved there and then to commit himself to the art of animation and move heaven and earth to join the Disney organization. As we shall see, Babbitt and Disney were to work together with rare success over the next decade until the early 1940s when there was a somewhat acrimonious parting of the ways.

Skeleton Dance was the first of the so-called Silly Symphonies, a series of cartoons initiated by Disney with the aim of allowing for extra experimentation in animation and subject matter in a way that was not possible in those Disney cartoons featuring popular characters. These cartoons could be more abstract than narrative in construction – adventures in shape and movement grouped around a theme, rather than a story featuring a main character. They undoubtedly extended the possibilities of animation, but at the time exhibitors were wary and wanted simply to cash in on the popularity of Disney's Mickey Mouse. For a while these adventurous cartoons had, rather ridiculously, to be advertised as 'Mickey Mouse presents a Walt Disney Silly Symphony.'

Skeleton Dance has no characters or plot but is simply a danse macabre. A graveyard comes alive at night and the emaciated corpses cavort merrily before climbing back into their graves. The idea had come from Carl Stalling who suggested a grisly frolic matched to 'March of the Dwarfs' from Grieg's *Lyric Suite*. Disney and Iwerks devised a story line and Iwerks did the animation. The scene is memorably set by silhouettes across a full moon; cats scurry away in terror and afterward a ballet for bones takes place. This music of the macabre anticipates Bernard Herrmann's percussive scoring of the skeleton duel in *The Seventh Voyage of Sinbad* (1958), animated by that great Disney admirer Ray Harryhausen, and even the remarkable coda of Shostakovich's death-haunted Symphony no. 15.

'Can't recommend it, too gruesome,' said the manager of a downtown LA theater, and his view was echoed by a number of disgruntled exhibitors. Yet few of Disney's shorts seem to retain the imaginative wit and freshness of this one. Moreover it is a work which highlights an important facet of the Disney cartoon – its affinity to ballet. 'The cartoon is the

ballet among the different forms of movie entertainment,' said Kurt Weill, 'and some of the scores written for Disney's pictures are fine examples of popular ballet music.' The close matching of music and movement, characteristic of *Skeleton Dance*, will lead in a logical line to the most balletic sequence in Disney and one of the most brilliant – the animation of the *Nutcracker* sequence in *Fantasia*.

The other element which *Skeleton Dance* emphasized and which was very characteristic of Disney at the time, was the element of the macabre. (One might recall that an equally gruesome short, *Hell's Bells*, was made by Disney in the same year.) Disney was not always the popular purveyor of sweetness and sentiment; he could also be a master of suspense. Nightmarish sequences also occur in *Snow White and the Seven Dwarfs* (1937), *Pinocchio* (1940) and *Fantasia* (1940). Those critics who have greeted recent Disney productions like *The Watcher in the Woods* (1981) and *Something Wicked This Way Comes* (1983) as aberrations seem to have forgotten the hefty dose of fright that often invigorated an early Disney short. These more recent films might be attempting a revival of the honorable tradition of wholehearted but wholesome horror in Disney, whose roots can be traced to the masterly romp *The Skeleton Dance*.

Flowers and Trees
1932

Although not the best-known nor the most popular of Disney cartoons, *Flowers and Trees* is a significant achievement. It was the first Disney cartoon to win an Oscar (or an Academy Award Certificate), triggering a remarkable sequence of success whereby a Disney short was to win the Oscar for best cartoon for the next seven years.

More importantly perhaps, *Flowers and Trees* became the first cartoon to be photographed in Technicolor's three-color process. Half of the film had already been shot when Technicolor announced that they had perfected a process which gave a much greater range of photographic color. In spite of the objections of his brother Roy, who was apprehensive about the additional expense, Disney decided to scrap the early black-and-white footage and reshoot the whole cartoon in color. One is reminded of Alfred Hitchcock's decision to add sound effects and reshoot some scenes with dialogue during the making of his silent film *Blackmail* (1929) once it became clear that the coming of sound was no flash in the pan. Disney was no less an innovator and sharp-eyed assessor

LEFT: Disney displays the Oscar he received for the creation of Mickey Mouse, and his 'Honorable Mention for Distinctive Achievement' Certificate which the Academy of Motion Picture Arts and Sciences awarded him for *Flowers and Trees*.

ABOVE RIGHT: The poster for *Flowers and Trees*, the first cartoon in full color in the history of animated film.

RIGHT: Fire in the forest in *Flowers and Trees*.

of trends than Hitchcock. He took a risk in using the new and expensive process, and it paid off handsomely.

In story terms, *Flowers and Trees* is a curious affair. A young male tree loves a young girl tree (drawn so seductively that it reminded one critic of Jean Harlow), but their romance is threatened by a rough, uncouth stump who tries to steal away the female. In a fit of pique at his rejection, the evil 'wood spirit' sets fire to the forest. Bluebells sound the alarm, prompting birds obligingly to poke holes in the clouds to produce rain. The villainous trunk is killed in the fire and the lovers marry, with a glowworm as their wedding ring.

The action is accompanied by snatches of classical music (Rossini, Schubert and Mendelssohn). Some of the themes and visual details – the awakening of the forest, the romantic rivalry, the forest fire – will be elaborated in later Disney, most notably in *Bambi* (1942). Color is used quite strikingly, not simply to describe and evoke but to express emotional intensity – something that would become characteristic of the use of color in Disney cartoons.

The film was successfully premiered at the prestigious Grauman's Chinese Theater in Los Angeles, attracting as much comment as the feature it was supporting, Irving Thalberg's version of Eugene O'Neill's *Strange Interlude* (1932) starring Clark Gable and Norma Shearer. After the film, Disney and Technicolor came to an agreement which gave Disney exclusive rights to the three-color process for cartoon productions until 1935 – which meant he had a considerable competitive edge over his rivals. After *Flowers and Trees* all the Silly Symphonies were in color (except for one), and, from being Mickey Mouse's poor relations, their status was considerably upgraded. The other Disney cartoon shorts to win Oscars during the 1930s were: *Three Little Pigs* (1933), *The Tortoise and the Hare* (1935), *Three Orphan Kittens* (1935), *Country Cousin* (1936), *The Old Mill* (1937), *Ferdinand the Bull* (1938) and *The Ugly Duckling* (1939).

Three Little Pigs
1933

Three Little Pigs is probably the most famous film cartoon ever made. Yet when it was completed the distributors had not been pleased. One even complained of being short-changed – 'The last cartoon Walt sent us was *Father Noah's Ark*, with dozens of animals. Now he gives us only four – three pigs and a wolf.' Even when it was premiered at Radio City Music Hall in New York, audiences were only mildly amused. However, when it was released more widely to neighborhood theaters, it was a tremendous success, sometimes earning top billing over the main feature. Although he was pleased with it, the film's overwhelming popularity took Disney completely by surprise. 'It was just another story to us,' he said later, 'and we were in there gagging it just like any other picture. After we heard all the shouting, we sat back and tried to analyze what made it good.'

Part of its popularity was undoubtedly attributable to its brilliant draughtsmanship. Norman 'Fergy' Ferguson (chief animator of Pluto) did the wolf; Dick Lundy did the scenes where the pigs danced to the theme song; Fred Moore did the pig footage; and Art Babbitt did some additional animation on the conclusion. Bert Gillett, who directed *Flowers and Trees*, was again in charge of direction. The use of color was both imaginative and funny, as in the moment when the wolf literally goes blue in the face in his unavailing attempt to blow the house down. Yet the main triumph was probably in characterization. Walt enthused to his brother Roy that he felt they had at last succeeded in getting human personality across in a cartoon feature, and his opinion was echoed by fellow animator and rival, Chuck Jones. 'That was the first time anybody ever brought characters to life in a cartoon,' Jones said. 'Before that, in things like *Steamboat Willie*, the villain was a big heavy guy and the hero was a little guy; everybody moved the same. But in *Three Little Pigs*, there were three characters who *looked* alike and *acted* differently; the way they moved is what made them what they were.'

Yet the most remarkable thing about the film was the interpretation that people seemed to put on it. Written by staff musician, Frank Churchill, the song 'Who's Afraid of the Big Bad Wolf?' became, in one critic's phrase, a national anthem overnight which enshrined the sentiments of an America determined to laugh the big bad wolf of the Depression out of its system. The three little pigs were seen as living proof of the effectiveness of President Roosevelt's exhortation to the American people to 'stick together,' and their cheery tones in

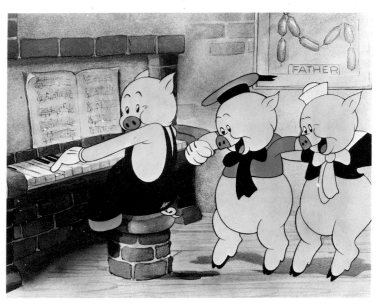

FAR LEFT ABOVE: The Wolf huffs and puffs to blow the house down.

LEFT ABOVE: The Wolf in sheep's clothing.

FAR LEFT BELOW: Who's afraid of the Big Bad Wolf? The three little pigs banish their fears in song.

LEFT BELOW: The Wolf finds things hotting up in the pigs' household.

RIGHT: Walt (left) looks on at the recording session of *Three Little Pigs*. Mary Moder, Pinto Colvig and Dorothy Compton are at the microphone; Frank Churchill is seated at the piano.

the height of adversity exemplified the kind of mood that could triumph over the huffing and puffing of wolfish adversity. 'I build my house of stones/I build my house of bricks/I have no chance to sing and dance/For work and play don't mix.' The message of such a lyric seems similar to that of another hugely popular film of the time, the musical *42nd Street* (1933) – everything comes to him who *works*. Both movies share a common theme in showing how teamwork and enterprise triumph; their success probably reflected a prevailing national mood.

Disney's genuine puzzlement over the success of *Three Little Pigs* and at the interpretations placed upon it, is quite revealing and interesting. Viewed today in the context of Disney's later output, the film has two qualities which rarely, if ever, resurfaced in future Disney films – contemporaneity and ambiguity. However obliquely and accidentally, *Three Little Pigs* was widely seen as a film that commented on contemporary society – never again was he to make a film of such immediate social relevance (unless one counts his propagandist war cartoons, and even then it is arguable). Also it was a rare example of a Disney film that could be (and has been) read in two distinctly different ways: in future even if there were differences in opinion over a film's aesthetic or entertainment value, there was no disagreement over what the film actually *meant*. *Three Little Pigs*, however, is different. Some critics take it as a film that exemplifies the spirit of Roosevelt's 'New Deal' America; others (perhaps influenced by Disney's well-publicized political conservatism) see it as an old-fashioned moral tract about the virtues of industriousness, self-reliance and preparedness – the successful pig is the one that takes out a form of life insurance. Maybe the ambiguity is rooted in Disney's personality at that time – an innately conservative man who was nevertheless progressive in his thinking and prepared to take risks.

It is curious how similar the film looks now to a hugely popular, modern film by a great admirer of Disney, which also comes out with a reassuring assertion of communal confidence after a period of political trauma in America – Steven Spielberg's *Jaws* (1975). Here again, we have three main characters defending their 'home' against a sharp-toothed marauder. In both cases the political theme is incidental, and the primal force of the films comes from the storytelling gifts of two master entertainers. Both films were also to inspire a plethora of sequels.

The message of the movie world to Disney was 'More pigs!' In one of the sequels, *Three Little Wolves* (1936), the wolf disguises himself improbably as Bo Peep (who is invariably treated disrespectfully in Disney), but is efficiently blown out of a cannon by the elder pig's Wolf Pacifier and lands up on a cloud. A similarly proficient Lie Detector will give the wolf a hard time in *The Practical Pig* (1939) after he has threatened two pigs who have not heeded advice and gone swimming ('Last one in is a pork sausage!'). The cartoons are immaculately drawn but they could not match the impact of the original. The point was neatly expressed by Disney when he said, 'How could we possibly top pigs – with pigs?'

The Band Concert
1935

Disney made many unforgettable cartoon shorts during the golden years between 1928 and 1942. For many *The Band Concert*, directed by Wilfred Jackson and the first Technicolor cartoon in which Mickey Mouse appears, is the best short of all during this period. For the distinguished film and art critic Gilbert Seldes it was Disney's 'greatest single work.'

The situation is simple. Mickey Mouse in a gorgeous scarlet coat is on the bandstand attempting to conduct a scintillating rendering of Rossini's 'William Tell Overture.' However, his concert is plagued by constant distractions that are alternately trivial, trying and then tumultuous. The trivial include a pestering bee which affects the precision of Mickey's conducting and a uniform so voluminous for Mickey that his sleeve keeps slipping over his baton. The trying comes in the form of Donald Duck who keeps interrupting the concert by playing 'Turkey in the Straw' on a tin whistle and sometimes getting the orchestra to follow him rather than Mickey. The tumultuous arrives in the shape of a tornado which suddenly transports the entire orchestra and concert into a midair whirlwind of color and dissonance before neatly depositing everyone back where they started from on the bandstand.

The comedy comes in many guises. The musical gags are particularly ingenious. For example it is the storm section of the Rossini overture that seems to precipitate the tornado; and the mixture of Rossini and 'Turkey in the Straw' at one stage produces an orchestral cacophony in the park that is remarkably similar to the playful, innovative dissonances of an orchestral composition by Charles Ives (who at that time had not yet been recognized as one of America's foremost composers). As the critic Joe Adamson remarked, one could take the whole film as a joke on the self-absorption of musicians. Not even an impending natural disaster can disturb Mickey's involvement in his music-making.

Perhaps the most striking feature of the film, though, is the contrast between the dedicated Mickey and the demonic Duck. For some time Disney had been commenting that Mickey had become something of a problem – because he was so beloved by the audience he was limited in what he could do, particularly regarding the extent of his naughtiness. From the mid-1930s, he becomes a sort of straight-man, at his best when attempting to maintain his dignity while all around are losing theirs. The belligerent, quick-tempered Donald Duck is another matter. Significantly it is Donald who is given the tune of 'Turkey in the Straw' which was Mickey's in *Steamboat Willie*, for it is Donald who has now taken over the anarchic antics that were formerly the province of the now comparatively austere and strait-laced Mickey. One can put the comparison in a slightly different way – whereas Mickey now has something of the grace and aristocratic air of an Astaire or a Fairbanks, Donald has all the cocky aggressiveness of James Cagney. Interestingly Donald has the last word – a triumph of Americana over high culture, and daring over dignity. One can see the influence of *The Band Concert* on the later classic, Tom and Jerry's *The Cat Concerto* (1946). If it is Disney's 'greatest single work,' then perhaps the reason is simple – in it both Mickey Mouse and Donald Duck give their greatest performances.

LEFT: The percussion section in *The Band Concert*.

ABOVE RIGHT: Donald makes his first disruptive entrance. However, not even a tornado will stop the band. Even though some members of the band are finally seen dangling from the trees surrounding the bandstand, they still complete their performance.

RIGHT: Mickey as ghostbuster in *Lonesome Ghosts* (1937), with Donald and Goofy as the other maladroit exorcists.

The Old Mill
1937

One of the reasons why the 1930s is such a fascinating and great period in the Disney story is the sense of excitement experienced then in the thrill of new discovery, either thematic or technical. This is true of *The Old Mill*, an Oscar-winning short directed by Wilfred Jackson. It was the first film by Disney to make use of the multiplane camera, a device for creating a sense of depth in animation by filming through up to six layers of glass backgrounds. It also gave a greater illusion of realism, which was always important to Disney. As a visual artist, he was always less attracted to the Cubist abstractions of Picasso or the Surrealism of Dali than to the naturalism of the great masters of the nineteenth century. Disney's idea of fantasy was not way-out imagination but the transformation of the familiar.

The Old Mill has no real plot. It is an observation of the behavior of animals who inhabit a deserted mill from sunset to sunrise. Proceedings are enlivened by the kind of vivid storm at which Disney animators excel, but mainly the events of the film reside in the close observation and animation of animal movement – the way ducks waddle, bats scatter or a frog catches a firefly. It is almost a cartoon anticipation of a Disney 'True Life Adventure.'

Its main interest is technical and also musical. The opening establishing shot is justly famous. The camera tracks in slowly, and gradually layer upon layer of detail is revealed, almost as if one were exploring more and more closely every inch of a great painting – a pond in the foreground, the mill itself, cows in the background of the shot, clouds which scud across the distant sky. Leigh Harline's lyrical music is closely matched to the action and, as many have pointed out, the film's structure is musical, essentially in sonata form. The opening shot of mill and inhabitants states the main theme; a subsidiary theme is expounded through a light-hearted, skittish observation of frogs in a pond; a storm inspires a dramatic development section; and a restatement of the main theme, with variations, is suggested by the shot which brings the film to its close, a backward-tracking camera movement which precisely reverses the way the film opened.

To describe *The Old Mill* in such a way perhaps gives the impression that it is more calculated and musically self-conscious than it actually is, but it might give an indication of the film's close organization which makes it so aesthetically satisfying. Curiously, Leigh Harline was the only musician during the great days of Disney to make his mark as a film composer outside of the Disney studio. (After winning an Oscar for the song 'When You Wish Upon a Star' from *Pinocchio*, he went freelance to score such varied and interesting pictures as George Stevens' *The More the Merrier* in 1943, Joseph Losey's *The Boy With Green Hair* in 1948 and Anthony Mann's *Man of the West* in 1958.) On another, elegiac note *The Old Mill* was probably the last of Disney's great Silly Symphonies. The experiments and innovations the series introduced were now to be incorporated into the feature-length fantasies. Someone by the name of Snow White was beckoning.

ABOVE: Lee Payne with Disney's first animation camera.

LEFT: A shot from *The Old Mill*. In its lyricism and absence of plot, this short looks ahead to *Fantasia*.

RIGHT: The multiplane camera in use here was perfected by Bill Garity and a team of technicians. It was also used throughout *The Old Mill*, and later extensively in *Pinocchio*.

CHAPTER TWO

With a Smile and a Song
Animated Features 1937-1967

The thirty years which separate Disney's first feature-length animated film (*Snow White and the Seven Dwarfs*, 1937) and the last on which he worked (*The Jungle Book*, 1967) saw immense fluctuations of fortune and aesthetic achievement in the Disney organization. In terms of artistry the first five years were the finest, producing a quintet of animated features between 1937 and 1942 whose level of excellence and excitement Disney was never to surpass. There is no dishonor in that – for neither has anyone else succeeded in surpassing Disney's achievements.

Yet those astonishingly creative years were also among Disney's most traumatic, involving financial anxiety and much else besides. Nowadays one recognizes the films produced during those years as popular classics, and tends to forget that, on first release, only *Snow White* made a large profit. One also tends to forget another film of some significance made by Disney during this period, *The Reluctant Dragon* (1941), in which three shorts – *Baby Weems, How to Ride a Horse* and *The Reluctant Dragon* – are intercut with a live-action tour of the studio hosted by the humorist Robert Benchley. The interest of the movie comes from its blend of live-action and animation, which was to increasingly preoccupy Disney over the next decade. It comes also from its unintentional irony. Benchley's illustration of the hard-working harmony of the Disney studio coincided with what the columnist Ezra Goodman was to describe as 'one of the most bitter labor strikes in Hollywood.'

The strike of 1941 involved half of Disney's employees, who were dissatisfied with working conditions, comparative wage structures, lay-offs and alleged lack of communication between management and staff. It must have been disconcerting for the producer of such fairy tales as *Snow White* and *Dumbo* to be greeted at his studio gates by militant pickets with placards proclaiming 'The Reluctant Disney' and 'Unfair not Funfair.' Disney's response was to identify Art Babbitt as the strike leader and arch trouble-maker and to

LEFT: Walt and Mickey Mouse merchandising.

ABOVE RIGHT: A relaxed moment for the Disney team in 1941: Bill Cottrell, one of Walt's most experienced employees, is on the right.

RIGHT: Picket lines outside the Disney gates during the strike of 1941.

LEFT: A shot from the 'Peter and the Wolf' section of *Make Mine Music* (1946), a layman's *Fantasia*.

BELOW LEFT: Studio personnel with Disney in 1934: from left to right, Clyde Geronimi, Albert Hurter, Art Babbitt, Hugh Hennesy, Wilfred Jackson, Gilles de Tremaudan, Walt, Dick Huemer, and Leigh Harline at the piano.

RIGHT: Donald Duck mocks the Nazi salute in *Der Fuehrer's Face* (1943), Disney's Chaplinesque satire of fascism.

BELOW RIGHT: Donald Duck looks for Latin American adventure in *Saludos Amigos* (1943).

sack him. This only inflamed the situation, and Disney was compelled to reinstate Babbitt. The strike ended after nine weeks, but Babbitt was to leave of his own accord two years later. By that time a number of talented animators had also gone, including Bill Tytla and a young animator John Hubley, who went on to help found a new production company, United Productions of America (UPA), whose product was soon to rival Disney's. Whether the strike and loss of personnel had any effect on the subsequent quality of the Disney product is impossible to say. Disney always maintained that his best animators were still with him after the dispute and no harm had been done. They were in excellent new studio conditions at Burbank and were raring to go. Nevertheless morale had been shaken, and it took some time to recover.

Another important factor at this time was America's involvement in World War II. It did not take long before the Disney studio became mobilized as part of the war effort, and began contributing numerous training cartoons for the Army, Navy, Air Force and other government departments on such themes as *Fog*, *Aircraft Carrier Landing Signals* and *Food Will Win the War*. As super-patriot and instinctive educator, Disney responded with enthusiasm to such commissions, though clearly the financial rewards would be minimal and would not ease their economic problems. Two famous and somewhat notorious movies came out of this period. One was *Der Fuehrer's Face* (1943), a furious farce in which Donald Duck dreams that he is working in a Nazi munitions factory. The other was *Victory Through Air Power* (1943), a fervent endorsement of Major Alexander de Seversky's controversial theories about strategic air-bombing. It impressed Winston Churchill but sent shivers down the spine of the sensitive critic James Agee, who began his review with the comment, 'I only hope Major de Seversky and Walt Disney know what they are talking about . . .'

Two features arose at this time from a goodwill tour of Latin America undertaken by Disney at the invitation of Nelson Rockefeller. The movies were partially funded by the State Department. *Saludos Amigos* (1943) consisted of four shorts on the theme of good neighborliness and featured,

among others, Donald Duck as a tourist in Peru and Goofy as a gaucho. *The Three Caballeros* (1945) was designed as a sort of sequel to *Saludos Amigos*, with Donald Duck joined this time by fellow caballeros Joe Carioca the Brazilian parrot, and Panchito the Mexican rooster. The highlight of the film was Ward Kimball's animation of the title song.

The war years had been disorientating for Disney as for many other American filmmakers, and it took him some years after the end of the war to find his artistic bearings. The films of the immediate postwar period suggest an uncertain search for a fresh identity, and are either uneven compilations or an uneasy combination of live-action and animation.

Make Mine Music (1946) is a poor man's *Fantasia*, an exercise in the animation of several styles of popular music, from hillbilly and jazz to Prokofiev's *Peter and the Wolf*. Its most famous sequence is 'Willie the Operatic Whale,' with vocals by Nelson Eddy. The Whale sings the roles of Pagliacci, Mephistopheles and Figaro before ascending to and serenading the inhabitants of a sort of heaven for mammals where the Pearly Gates have a 'Sold Out' notice draped over them. *Song*

of the South (1946) is a less eccentric, more earnest venture, combining live-action footage and cartoon inserts, and with James Baskett as Uncle Remus telling the story of Br'er Rabbit and Br'er Fox. The movie may have been an influence on Steven Spielberg's *The Color Purple* (1985), but nowadays it looks patronizing and is best remembered for Gregg Toland's spanking photography and for the popular hit song 'Zip-A-Dee-Doo-Dah.'

Disney's following features are a rather undistinguished package. 1947 saw the release of *Fun and Fancy Free*, memorable for an episode involving Bongo the circus bear. 'Mickey and the Beanstalk' which followed is interesting mainly because Mickey Mouse is mainly voiced by Jim Macdonald and not by Walt who was too busy to produce the recordings. *Melody Time* (1948) follows the adventures of Pecos Bill and features Roy Rogers and the Sons of the Pioneers. *The Adventures of Ichabod and Mr Toad* (1949) interprets two wildly contrasting stories, the tale of Ichabod Crane (from Washington Irving's *The Legend of Sleepy Hollow*) which is sung and spoken by Bing Crosby, and the tale of Mr Toad (from Kenneth Grahame's *The Wind in the Willows*) which is narrated by Basil Rathbone. Add to these films Disney's tame rural drama, *So Dear to My Heart* (1949), and one can see that the five years after the war were arguably Disney's creative nadir. The studio was ticking over without any real sense of direction. However, the enormous success of *Cinderella* (1950) was to prove a massive fillip.

Because of Disney's diversification into full-scale features, it was inevitable that there would be some falling-off in both the number and the quality of imagination of the cartoon shorts. Nevertheless stars like Mickey, Donald and Pluto were kept going, and often excelled themselves. In *Mr Mouse Takes a Trip* (1940), Mickey and Pluto hide in a most amusing and ingenious way from a zealous ticket inspector who has railway signals on his watch and who intimidatingly punches holes in the tickets with his teeth. In *Bone Trouble* (1940) Pluto has to hide from a large dog while visiting a carnival.

He enters the Hall of Mirrors where at first he is terrified by the distortion. He then proceeds to do impersonations of a camel, crocodile, kangaroo and seal – all of which are brilliantly animated by Jack Kinney. Among the new characters were two chirpy chipmunks, Chip 'n' Dale, but although they moved in on Mickey and Pluto's habitation in the Oscar-nominated *Squatter's Rights* (1946), they never really moved in with the same success on the general public's affection.

Disney kept the shorts department going, partly because he did not like to dismantle an operation that was running smoothly and at modest profit, and partly because it provided a useful training ground for future feature-film animators. As the cartoons of the famous characters dwindled – Mickey Mouse made his last film appearance in Disney's lifetime in 1953 – so the Disney shorts tended to become one-off special projects. Two good examples are Hamilton Luske's *Ben and Me* (1953) which tells the story of a church mouse called Amos who leaves home and his family of 26 ('it was one less mouse to feed'), ultimately both inventing bifocals and influencing the career of Benjamin Franklin; and Ward Kimball's Oscar-winning *Toot, Whistle, Plunk and Boom* (1953), an off-beat history of music, made in CinemaScope. This tradition was continued in the 1960s with a memorable series of 'Winnie the Pooh' cartoons. Wolfgang Reitherman directed *Winnie the Pooh and the Honey Tree* (1966) and *Winnie the Pooh and the Blustery Day* (1968), and John Lounsbery directed *Winnie the Pooh and Tigger Too* (1974). The Americanization of AA Milne was a little incongruous, though Sterling Holloway's voicing of Pooh as a sort of benign, befuddled WC Fields is very endearing.

Nevertheless, from the 1930s onward and until the idea of Disneyland became a gleam in his eye, it was the feature-length cartoons on which Disney expended most of his creative and organizational energies. To assess how well that time was spent, one need only observe how often the movies have been revived since they were initially released. In this particular field nobody has surpassed Walt Disney.

LEFT: The Walt Disney Studio in February 1930. From left to right, Dick Lundy, Tom Palmer, Johnny Cannon, Dave Hand, Bert Gillett, Wilfred Jackson, Bert Lewis, Walt, Les Clark, Ben Sharpsteen, Norman Ferguson, Floyd Gottfredson and Jack King.

RIGHT: The 'Mickey and the Beanstalk' animated sequence from *Fun and Fancy Free* (1947).

BELOW LEFT AND RIGHT: The techniques of animation: painting the background, and inking in and painting the characters.

Snow White and the Seven Dwarfs
1937

When asked in an interview to single out the quality that made Walt Disney so exceptionally successful, Art Babbitt replied, 'He was a great gambler.' Undoubtedly Disney's greatest gamble was *Snow White and the Seven Dwarfs*, the first ever full-length animated feature which, as costs soared, began to be known in the industry as 'Disney's Folly.' It cost $1.5 million, took three years to make and involved the work of nearly six hundred artists who produced an estimated two million drawings. If it had failed, the history of Walt Disney Productions, and of animation, and even of movies generally, might well have been very different. But its premiere at the Carthay Circle Theater in Los Angeles in December 1937 was a triumph and, on release in 1938, *Snow White* made over $8 million, the biggest take of any movie since DW Griffith's *The Birth of a Nation* (1915).

Disney had thought of doing an animated feature-length film as early as 1934, partly for economic reasons (the profits from shorts were strictly limited) and partly for creative ones (he wanted more room in his movies for the exploration of character and style). He might have chosen the subject of Snow White because the first film he could remember as having made a deep impression on him was a silent version of the fairy tale which he had seen in Kansas City in 1917. Once

he had made up his mind he threw himself into the project with that meticulous, obsessive sense of detail that had become Disney's hallmark.

He rapidly realized that a film on this scale would represent quite a challenge, for they were attempting many things that they had not tried before. For example Disney's animators were not used to animating the human form; the short film *The Goddess of Spring* (1934) was mainly designed as an

GROUP: GET YOUR FILL O' THE JOYS THAT COME WITH THE MUSIC IN YOUR SOUP!

experiment so that the animators could practice this art and apply what they learned to *Snow White*. Another consideration was the matter of tempo. 'We started out gaily in the fast tempo that is the special technique of short subjects,' said Disney. 'But that wouldn't do; we soon realized there was a danger of wearing out the audience.' Disney also had to redefine his sense of structure, and regretfully he had to cut two sequences on which Ward Kimball animated – a dwarf soup-concert, and a scene where the dwarfs build a bed for Snow White – because he felt they slowed the momentum of the narrative down too much.

Numerous names for the dwarfs were devised and discussed before final agreement was reached on the magnificent seven: Doc, Dopey, Bashful, Sleepy, Happy, Grumpy and Sneezy (originally called Jumpy). Disney was concerned that each should have his own distinctive personality and mannerisms. For the animator this would affect his drawing

of such things as the spacing of the hands, different head movements, walk and speed of reaction. Small wonder that the song routine 'Heigh-ho, heigh-ho, it's home from work we go' took six months to animate. The artists mainly in charge of the dwarfs were Freddy Moore, Bill Tytla, Fred Spencer and Frank Thomas.

Snow White and the Prince were under the overall responsibility of Hamilton Luske and Grim Natwick. Disney's conception of the Prince (who might bring Snow White to life but never really does the same for himself) was as a 'Douglas Fairbanks type.' Snow White, according to Disney, was a 'Janet Gaynor type.' As a guide to the animators a young dancer, Marge Belcher, was hired to rehearse Snow White's movements. She was later to become Art Babbitt's wife and, after their divorce, achieved fame as Marge Champion of the dancing duo, Marge and Gower Champion. For the voice of Snow White, Disney hired a young opera

ABOVE LEFT: A sketch of Grumpy.

LEFT: A detail from the dwarf-soup concert. Regretfully, Disney decided to cut this scene from the final film.

ABOVE: One of the estimated two million drawings involved in the film's preparation.

ABOVE RIGHT: A sketch of Doc.

RIGHT: An image that immediately crystallizes the innocence of Snow White and, by implication, the wickedness of the Queen in wanting Snow White killed.

singer, Adriana Caselotti (one of the people who auditioned for this job and was turned down was a young Deanna Durbin). Disney saw the Wicked Queen as a cross between Lady Macbeth and the Big Bad Wolf. Art Babbitt did the animation of her as the Queen, skillfully keeping the characterization very controlled, in contrast to the broad style for the dwarfs. The animation for the Queen's disguise as an old pedlar was the responsibility of Norman Ferguson. Pretty

blood-chilling and frightening she was too, although the critic Otis Ferguson was to complain that she looked rather too much like actor Lionel Barrymore in drag.

The movie is less grim than the Grimm fairy tale on which it is based, but it is still tense as well as tender, and one of the strengths of the film is its compelling narrative – mirth, music and murder are all artfully mixed. After learning from a contrite huntsman that her stepmother, the Queen, wishes to kill

FAR LEFT ABOVE: Snow White at the wishing well, where she will meet the handsome Prince.

LEFT ABOVE: Snow White's first glimpse of the dwarfs' cottage.

LEFT: 'I know – we'll clean the house and surprise them. Then maybe they'll let me stay.' Snow White and her forest friends do the dwarfs' dusting and cleaning.

ABOVE: Snow White meets the dwarfs.

RIGHT: The Queen with her casket which, as the design implies, she thinks will hold the heart of Snow White. The Magic Mirror will soon disillusion her.

her because of her beauty, Snow White flees through the forest, the whole of surrounding nature becoming infected by her fear. Equally suspenseful is a chase later in the film when the disguised Queen who has poisoned Snow White with a red apple, is pursued in a storm by the enraged dwarfs, and justice is delivered in the form of a bolt of lightning. Between these highlights of excitement the mood is lightened by comedy and song. The dwarfs are all marvelously characterized; there is an enchanting scene when Snow White and her friends from the forest first arrive at the dwarfs' house and begin cleaning, squirrels using their tails as brushes, birds flying about with sheets to shake them dry. The songs by Frank Churchill and Larry Morey include such classics as 'Some Day My Prince Will Come,' 'Whistle While You Work'

and 'With a Smile and a Song.' Even Steven Spielberg's *Gremlins*, 1984, are entranced by 'Heigh-ho, Heigh-ho.' The score was much admired when the film was first released, and it is perhaps not said often enough that Disney's animated features are among the screen's best musicals.

The combination of elements works ideally in *Snow White*. The intensity of its images grips the imagination – the bright red of that poisoned apple seems to glow demonically. The story-telling, with its Sleeping Beauty theme of a virginal young girl awakening into love and womanhood, possesses a fairy-tale purity. And curiously the film succeeds in conveying a feeling of emotional authenticity, as the twisted sexual jealousy of the Wicked Queen communicates with the raw conviction of high-class melodrama.

HIS FIRST FULL LENGTH FEATURE PRODUCTION

Walt Disney's
Snow White
and the Seven Dwarfs
in the Marvelous
MULTIPLANE TECHNICOLOR

©WDP   Distributed by RKO Radio Pictures, Inc.

When asked once to sum up the *Snow White* venture Disney quoted Webster's definition of 'adventure': 'risk, jeopardy; encountering of hazardous enterprise; a daring feat; a bold undertaking in which the issue hangs on unforeseen events.' Disney was indubitably one of the cinema's great adventurers. *Snow White* was a breathtaking risk, but Disney never flinched from fulfilling his vision, and in the end his success was as spectacular as it was deserved. In addition to the public acclaim, two things must have particularly gladdened his heart – a special Oscar presentation to him by Shirley Temple of one normal and seven dwarf-sized statuettes; and the summary by that eminent American critic and filmmaker Pare Lorentz of Disney's achievement – 'the one artist in Hollywood turning out his masterpiece.'

FACING PAGE TOP LEFT: The Wicked Queen, disguised as an old pedlar, offers Snow White the bright red poisoned apple.

FACING PAGE TOP RIGHT: Snow White in her coffin of gold, the dwarfs keeping vigil at her side. The Prince approaches to break the spell.

ABOVE LEFT: My Prince has come: Snow White is revived.

ABOVE: The poster for *Snow White*.

FACING PAGE BOTTOM: The glittering premiere of *Snow White*, at the Carthay Circle Theater in Hollywood.

LEFT: Walt receives his Oscars – one normal size, and seven dwarfs – from Shirley Temple. Before going on stage, she said to him: 'Don't be nervous, Mr Disney.'

Pinocchio
1940

Pinocchio cost over $2 million to make and yet it took only $3 million at the box-office, a disappointing performance after the runaway success of *Snow White*. '*Pinocchio* might have lacked the heart appeal of *Snow White*,' mused Disney afterward, 'but technically and artistically it was superior.' Most critics would now agree with that.

Pinocchio is based on the fantasy by Carlo Collodi, which presented a lot of problems for Disney and his team. It was relatively straightforward to hack out an acceptable narrative from the original, and the movie concentrated essentially on three main episodes from Collodi's tale – from Pinocchio's brief career as an actor, the film went on to cover his traumatic trip to Pleasure Island, and then his underwater search for Geppetto, the 'father' whose desire for a son has brought him to life. It was much more difficult to decide the best way of animating Pinocchio, who had been entrusted to the capable hands of Frank Thomas, Milt Kahl and Ollie Johnston. It was obvious he had to be made more sympathetic than in the original story, but how could that be done without depriving him of personality? Also, should he be animated like a puppet or like a small boy? Before these problems were ironed out Disney halted production, and only resumed when problems of design and development had been solved.

One way round the woodenness of Pinocchio's character was to surround him with vivid supporting characters who would play off his passivity. In particular this meant building up the character of Jiminy Cricket who, in the original, is casually squashed by Pinocchio at a very early stage. In Disney's version he is the voice of Pinocchio's conscience, a witty womanizer, a streetwise satirist with the cheek of a Charlie Chaplin, and most importantly, the main audience

ABOVE LEFT: A typical Disney opening: Jiminy Cricket introduces us to the classic book *Pinocchio*.

LEFT: Geppetto's workshop. This shot reveals the intricacy, detail and craftsmanship of Disney's artists and designers.

ABOVE: Pinocchio, Geppetto, Figaro the cat and Jiminy Cricket.

RIGHT: Pinocchio is taken for a walk.

ABOVE LEFT: Honest John the fox, Gideon the cat and the coachman meet at the Red Lobster Inn to hatch their wicked plans to make money out of Pinocchio.

LEFT: It is as plain as the nose on Pinocchio's face that he is lying to the Blue Fairy.

ABOVE: One of the film's most extraordinary images: Jiminy floats past the eye of the whale.

RIGHT: Geppetto carries the unconscious Pinocchio after the puppet has proved his bravery and unselfishness by saving the old man's life.

LEFT: Inside the whale: Geppetto is trapped inside the belly of Monstro.

RIGHT: Mind the jaws: Pinocchio and Geppetto cause Monstro to sneeze so that they can sail out of his mouth on a raft.

BELOW RIGHT: Another vital department in the Disney team: creating the sound effects.

identification figure in the movie. It is he who will expound the film's philosophy in the song 'When You Wish Upon a Star' (which was to win an Oscar for its composers Leigh Harline and Ned Washington) and one might say that, in this song, he is expressing the philosophical creed behind the whole of Disney entertainments. The animation of the character was entrusted mainly to Ward Kimball who was given the assignment after going in to see Disney with the intention of resigning (after his work on *Snow White* had been cut); Kimball was so overwhelmed by Disney's enthusiasm for Jiminy's character that he forgot the reason for his visit.

The good characters in the film – Pinocchio, Jiminy Cricket, the Blue Fairy and Geppetto – are all portrayed very affectionately, particularly Geppetto, characterized mainly by Art Babbitt. But it is the villains who stand out – a patrol of male authority figures who seem determined to blight Pinocchio's growth to humanity. One wonders if Disney saw any parallels with his own earlier life in the story – the restrictions, the possible temptations. Like Disney, Pinocchio has a rather ineffectual father figure. He is pointed in the direction of show business, but his guides are a duplicitous duo, the fox J Worthington Foulfellow and the cat Gideon, and they direct him to the tawdry 'Stromboli Marionette Show.' In the contrast between the conscientious Geppetto who is a perfectionist at his craft, and the theater manager Stromboli who merely wants to make money, it is hard not to sense a Disney comment on the ethics of the Hollywood film industry – the rival claims of art and commercialism. One should remember that at this stage in his career Disney's film operations were far from being on a firm financial footing and he was often regarded by the industry as an arty individualist working somewhat outside the mainstream.

Pinocchio's terrors intensify when he encounters the evil coachman who transports Pinocchio and a delinquent boy, Lampwick, to the unbridled delights of Pleasure Island but later insists on exacting a terrible price (it is surprising how in so many details *Pinocchio* anticipates a Disney production of more than forty years later, *Something Wicked This Way Comes*). Because they act like jackasses, Pinocchio and Lampwick literally become jackasses in a terrifying transformation scene, and they are only rescued by the timely intervention of Jiminy. The final threat is Monstro the Whale who has already swallowed Geppetto whole. In entering the Whale to rescue his 'father' Pinocchio will fulfill the promise of the Blue Fairy: To make Geppetto's wish [for a son] to come true, you must prove yourself brave, truthful and unselfish. And some day you will be a *real* boy.'

Pinocchio is not a comedy with a few scary moments – it is rather a nightmare that is illuminated with a few flashes of humor. It shares a lot of similarities with *Frankenstein*, notably the 'unnatural' bringing to life of a creature who will then have to contend with a world of often monstrous cruelty. Whether Disney had this parallel in mind is not clear, though it is interesting that the vulnerability of Pinocchio and of Boris Karloff's monster in *Frankenstein* is initially indicated in the same way – their sensitivity to fire. Certainly it is an animated feature permeated with fear and with images that could well disturb children, notably the way Pinocchio's nose lengthens when he tells lies to the Blue Fairy.

For connoisseurs of multiplane camera animation, there is a breathtaking opening panning shot that takes us over the village and to Geppetto's shop; and lovers of Disney's comic detail will delight in that moment when, overjoyed at Pinocchio's recovery, Figaro the cat jumps wildly into the goldfish bowl and gives Cleo the goldfish a great big kiss. It is probably the most dramatic of Disney's animated features, showing the possibilities for animation of dealing with primal human emotions and adult themes and yet of also involving audiences of all ages in its adventure. For sheer technique *Pinocchio* has never been surpassed. As Jiminy Cricket exclaims when he realizes that the Blue Fairy has brought Pinocchio to life, 'Whew! What they can't do these days!'

Fantasia
1940

Artistic travesty or grand adventure? *Fantasia* is the most controversial of Disney's great cartoons. Great music is set to animated illustration (or the other way round) in an endeavor either to bring a mass audience to the classics or an art audience to Disney. There is no doubt that *Fantasia* introduced an enormous number of people to classical music and many music critics have acknowledged Disney's film as a formative influence. There are also those who have never been able to forgive him.

Fantasia grew out of Disney's desire to rejuvenate the career of Mickey Mouse. While attending a party Disney met the great conductor Leopold Stokowski who proved as keen as Disney himself to bring his art to the masses. Disney mentioned that he was thinking of starring Mickey in a cartoon interpretation of Dukas' *The Sorcerer's Apprentice*, and Stokowski (a great Mickey fan) not only offered to conduct the music but suggested that this concept of fitting animation to music might be extended to other suitable compositions. The idea took hold of Disney and soon a team had been assigned to choose music that could stimulate effective animation.

The range of music considered was generally in the field of popular classics that contained something of a storyline as well as obvious pictorial associations.

This principle of selection was not adhered to strictly, although the movie is arguably at its most effective when it is. The film begins with Stokowski's arrangement of Bach's *Toccata and Fugue*, which is an animated exercise in abstraction, and ends with Schubert's *Ave Maria*, which becomes a study in ponderously prolonged piety. It was Stokowski who suggested the use of Stravinsky's *Rite of Spring* in response to Disney's desire to depict the creation of the earth, and the imagery of primitive landscapes and prehistoric monsters is as bizarrely fascinating as Stokowski's brazen rejigging of the score. Stravinsky, the only living composer to be represented in *Fantasia*, is said not to have liked Disney's interpretation of his score – but then he was not keen on Herbert von Karajan's either.

The most heavily criticized section of the film was the visual interpretation of Beethoven's *Pastoral* Symphony ('when listening to Beethoven,' said Leonard Bernstein in a 1973 Harvard Lecture on the symphony, 'try not to think of those Disney nymphs and centaurs'). It looks very coy, and is only redeemed by a good storm and by Stokowski's briskly lilting performance which dispatches the symphony in just

BELOW LEFT: The camera prepares to film conductor Leopold Stokowski in *Fantasia*.

RIGHT: Disney's version of the ballet: the Alligator Dance Company cavort to 'Dance of the Hours.'

BELOW: The barbaric rhythms of Stravinsky's *Rite of Spring* are visually interpreted as representing the bestial struggle of prehistoric monsters.

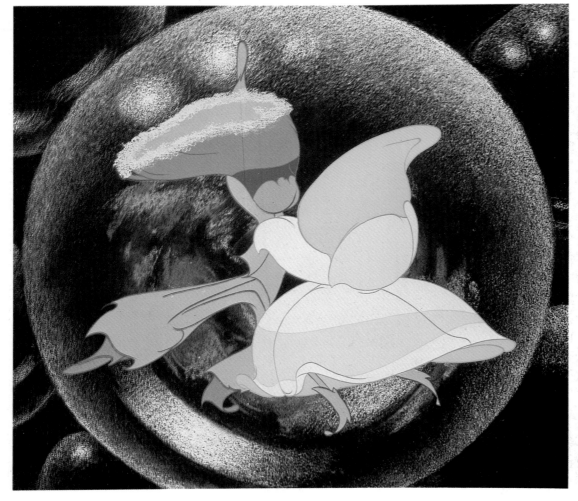

ABOVE: Art Babbitt's delectable dancing mushrooms in the 'Chinese Dance' from the 'Nutcracker Suite,' in *Fantasia*.

LEFT: The 'Russian Dance' from 'The Nutcracker': a thistle in the form of a Cossack bursts out of a large bubble.

ABOVE RIGHT: Hippo and alligator in a pas-de-deux from 'Dance of the Hours.'

RIGHT: The 'Waltz of the Flowers,' where seeds become ballerinas.

LEFT: The 'Night on a Bald Mountain' sequence in *Fantasia* shows good triumphing over evil.

BELOW: Mickey as the Sorcerer's Apprentice – the idea that inspired the film.

RIGHT: Mickey rapidly getting out of his depth, as the brooms and pails become a malevolent production line.

over twenty minutes. The pure music of Bach and Schubert is also ill-served by distracting visual elaboration.

On the other hand, there are moments of sheer brilliance. The ungainly routine of the hippos in the 'Dance of the Hours' is a superb parody of ballet and Busby Berkeley and could stand alone as a Silly Symphony. Art Babbitt's magnificent animation of the dancing Chinese mushrooms in Tchaikovsky's *Nutcracker Suite* was described at the time by Chuck Jones as the 'happiest, most perfect single sequence ever done in animated cartoons, perhaps in motion pictures.' Modeled on footage acted out by Bela Lugosi, Bill Tytla's drawing of Chernabog in Mussorgsky's *Night on a Bald Mountain* is genuinely frightening. Jim Algar directed *The Sorcerer's Apprentice* section and it is a classic Mickey Mouse sequence, in which the music is brilliantly matched to Mickey's screen persona, particularly his tendency to indulge in fantasy (as in a 1936 cartoon like *Thru the Mirror*), and to initiate situations that get out of control.

It is often said that Mickey Mouse was Disney's alter ego, and his role in *Fantasia*, as a would-be sorcerer whose spells get a little out of hand, tends to confirm that. The critics were divided about the film and the public stayed away, possibly fearing that Disney had made an art movie and, like Huck Finn's Aunt Sally, was trying to 'sivilize me and I can't stand it.' Actually nothing was farther from Disney's mind. What he was attempting in *Fantasia* was the same as in his other cartoons – to extend the boundaries of animation. In *Fantasia* there are innovations in film structure and stereo sound, and a new fusion of image and music. Over the years the movie has gone into profit and acquired an audience and, more recently, also a new digitally recorded soundtrack (though Irwin Kostal's performances lack the personality of Stokowski's). Its mixture of fairy tale and grotesque still looks strange, and even those who do not take exception to the idea of putting pictures to music find the level of inspiration very uneven. When it fails to work it is embarrassing, but at its best *Fantasia* will, as its publicity claimed, 'amaze ya.'

LEFT: A high point in the career of both Mickey Mouse and Leopold Stokowski: they shake each other's hands.

ABOVE RIGHT: The poster for *Fantasia*. On a re-release in 1946, the publicity was to claim: '*Fantasia* will amaze ya.'

RIGHT: Disney merchandising: *Fantasia* spin-offs of books and scores.

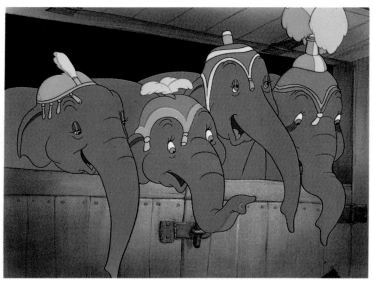

Dumbo
1941

There is a moment in Steven Spielberg's *1941* (1979), when a general (Robert Stack) sits laughing and crying through a showing of *Dumbo* while outside all hell is breaking loose. It is a joke with a number of ramifications. It pokes fun at the childlike simplicity of the general, and draws a comic contrast between the charm emanating inside the theater and the chaos raging outside. It is a reminder of Spielberg's own affection for Disney's films and also of the period in which *Dumbo* was made. It arrived to banish the blues at a time when America was nervously readying itself for war.

Based on a book by Helen Aberson and Harold Pearl, *Dumbo* is the story of an elephant who suffers humiliation because of his abnormally large ears but who becomes a star when he discovers he can fly. It only runs to sixty-four minutes; Disney resisted pressure to make it longer, feeling it worked perfectly at that length, and he was right. It cost a fraction of the budgets of *Snow White*, *Fantasia* and *Pinocchio*, but it doubled its investment at the box-office.

Dumbo is one of Disney's most direct, appealing and effective movies, with a pacy narrative that has no distractions. It is perhaps one of his most American tales. Dumbo is at times presented almost as a Depression hero ('socially he's washed up . . .' says his friend Timothy Q Mouse to some crestfallen crows) – down on his luck through no fault of his own. The story also shares a common theme with the American classic, *Pudd'nhead Wilson* by Mark Twain, which is also about a 'dumbo' whose unsuspected talent turns an erstwhile contemptuous community on its ears.

It is one of the most affectionately characterized of Disney's movies. The stork who delivers Dumbo is superbly voiced by Sterling Holloway and delightfully conceived by

FACING PAGE TOP LEFT: The circus moves on to another town.

FACING PAGE TOP RIGHT: Some of the best humor of the film comes from the older elephants.

ABOVE: The cold shoulder for Dumbo when he has been made a clown.

LEFT: Mother and Dumbo, whose early life together will alternate between painful separation and joyous reunion.

BELOW: Wolfgang Reitherman works on the drawings of Timothy Mouse.

LEFT: Dumbo is befriended by Timothy Mouse who assures him that 'lots of people with big ears are famous.'

BELOW: As revenge for their treatment of Dumbo, Timothy frightens the other elephants.

RIGHT: Dumbo finds he can fly.

BELOW RIGHT: 'Pink Elephants on Parade.' Part of the superb delirium scene after Dumbo and Timothy have inadvertently drunk champagne.

animator Art Babbitt as a Western Union messenger, insisting on singing 'Happy Birthday' and getting Mrs Jumbo to sign a receipt. Equally attractive are the fiercely protective Mrs Jumbo, Timothy Q Mouse as the hero's friend and support, and some naughty elephants (animated by Bill Tytla and John Lounsbery). The affectionate tone extends itself into the smallest detail, such as the moment when a kangaroo transforms itself into a rocking-chair to rock her baby to sleep, or when a gorilla fiercely shows its strength on a parade by ripping out a bar of its cage and then sheepishly returns it as if apologizing for its act of vandalism.

There are moments of pathos too. In a painful scene Mrs Jumbo, after defending Dumbo from some odious brats, is forceably removed from her child and locked in a cage. A sequence where the circus tent is assembled during a storm is genuinely impressive and exciting. The only dubious element perhaps is the presentation of the crows as Negro caricatures, though their song in praise of Dumbo, 'When I See an Elephant Fly,' is such an exuberant spiritual that the buoyancy banishes any suspicion of bigotry.

The most extraordinary sequence in *Dumbo*, however – and arguably the most extraordinary sequence in Disney – occurs when Dumbo and Timothy drink from a bucket which they think contains water but has actually been accidentally topped up with the clowns' champagne. What follows is a drunken reverie at least the equal of the Oscar-winning cartoon *The Country Cousin*; and a surreal nightmare in which pink elephants metamorphose themselves into Arab belly dancers, waltzers, nightclub singers and finally a peaceful cloud formation. This 'Pink Elephants on Parade' sequence was created by a number of different animators including Norman Ferguson, Karl van Leuven, Hicks Lokey, Howard Swift and Ken O'Connor and it is one of the high points of animation art: not even the delirium scene of Wilder's *The Lost Weekend* (1945) and the cartoon nightmare of Hitchcock's *Vertigo* (1958) have surpassed it in evoking the effect of alcohol and hallucination. From the nightmare, however, Dumbo will wake up into the American Dream.

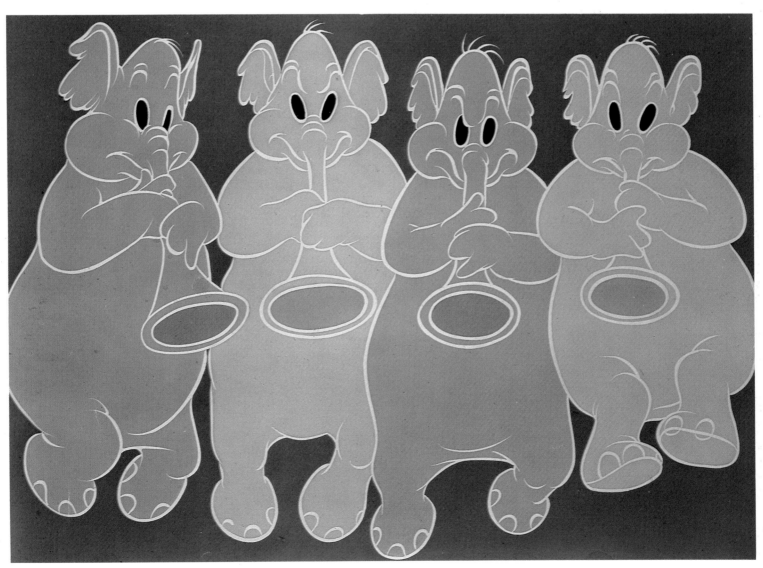

Bambi

1942

The making of the film *Bambi*, from inception to full maturation, seems to have been as fraught with difficulties as the eponymous fawn's own progress from birth to becoming prince of the forest. Disney had purchased the rights to Felix Salten's book in 1937 and preparatory work had begun immediately. However, what with interruptions ranging from technical difficulties to the animators' strike of 1941, the film was not finally released until 1942.

When it did appear the response was disappointing. America's wartime audience required something either real or uplifting, and the remote and strangely introspective *Bambi* was neither. Yet it was too real for some critics. An animator on the movie had remarked that Disney 'might as well have gone out and taken pictures of real deer, that was the quality he was driving for in the animation'; and it was well known that deer were being kept on the Disney lot for observation and that artists involved on the film were required to attend classes on the finer points of drawing animals. Was this attention to detail a violation of the deliberate unreality and fantasy of the cartoon? Some thought so. What Disney seems to have been doing in *Bambi* is nudging the cartoon in the direction of documentary. Of all his animated features this is the one that most closely anticipates the True-Life Adventures series of a decade later.

Yet the years seem to have lent an added enchantment to *Bambi*, whose reputation has grown as the film's originality has become more apparent. It is interesting to read the screenwriter William Goldman (*Butch Cassidy and the Sundance Kid*, 1969; *All the President's Men*, 1976) on *Bambi* and his impressions on re-viewing the film forty years after it was released. According to Goldman, in comparison with *Star Wars*, which has gone stale in five years, *Bambi* looks fresher than ever. In comparison with *The Deer Hunter* (1979) which looks like a comic-book movie, says Goldman, *Bambi* 'has a terrifying sense of life to it, and not life as we like it to be.'

Goldman's point about the 'terror' in *Bambi* is well taken. As he suggests, the brutal killing of the mother midway through *Bambi* is a shock effect every bit as effective for its

LEFT: Eric Larson, one of the five chief animators who worked on *Bambi*.

ABOVE RIGHT: An art class in progress, as *Bambi* strives for an unprecedented cartoon realism. From left to right, Murray McLennan, Bernie Wolf, Rico Lebrun, Eric Larson (drawing) study one of the deer being kept at the Disney studio during the making of the film.

RIGHT: Bambi, who will grow into the Prince of the Forest.

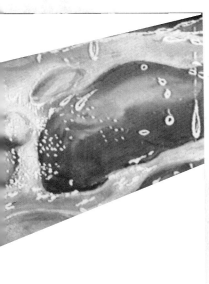

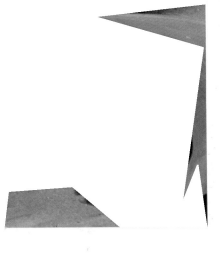

FACING PAGE TOP LEFT: In spring a young skunk's mind lightly turns to thoughts of love.

FACING PAGE TOP RIGHT: Two of the most endearing characters in *Bambi*: Flower the skunk and Thumper the rabbit.

LEFT: April showers.

TOP LEFT: Bambi alone in the snow-covered forest.

TOP RIGHT: Bambi and his father in the snow.

ABOVE: The fight for Faline.

time as Hitchcock's famous shower murder in *Psycho* (1960). *Bambi* might have the reputation of being a fey little fable about fawns, but it is a basically serious film about the changing seasons and the endless cycle of life from birth to death. It is also about the contrast between the compassion of animals and the inhumanity of humans. Although no human figure is seen in the film, man's presence is felt as a violation of nature, and the most ominous line in the movie, which causes panic, is: 'Man . . . was in the forest.' Of all Disney movies *Bambi* is the one that is closest in spirit to the poetry of William Blake. It is a Song of Innocence, but there is the constant awareness that Experience lurks threateningly in the wings.

A long opening panning shot through the forest carries us to the heart of the film's setting and introduces us to the birth of Bambi, which is very delicately drawn. Bambi is brought up by his mother, but when he first meets his father, the Great Prince of the Forest, the effect is as awesome as the young boy's first sight of the hero in George Stevens' *Shane* (1953). Was Stevens thinking of *Bambi* when he shot that

LEFT: The forest fire threatens.

RIGHT: Sheet music from Disney's films, a reminder of the importance of songs to the success of a Disney cartoon.

BELOW: A typically beautiful composition from *Bambi*, perhaps Disney's finest nature poem.

opening scene? It is worth remembering that our first glimpse of Shane's approach to the farm is an extraordinary shot – the antlers of a deer neatly frame the scene, which depicts the deer turning its head toward the figure that can be seen in the distance.

Winter comes, giving the opportunity for imaginative slapstick involving two of Disney's most likeable supporting characters, Flower the skunk and Thumper the rabbit. The way Thumper taps snow out of his ear with his foot is the kind of behavioral quirk that Disney will attempt to capture in his future wildlife films. The pursuit of Bambi's mother who is killed even as she ensures the safety of Bambi, is a tremendously powerful scene – a reminder that there is tragedy in Disney as well as sentiment. The appearance here of the Prince of the Forest, silhouetted in the snowstorm as he breaks the news of the tragedy to Bambi, remains justly memorable as it achieves an effect of genuine grandeur.

A deft change of mood is initiated by the coming of spring, and a characteristically crotchety Owl (a variation of the character will reappear in *Sword in the Stone*) warns of the dangers of being 'twitterpated,' that is, falling in love. Bambi is entranced by Faline and has a savage fight over her with a rival, a black struggle periodically illuminated by flashes of lightning. Then the crows come as harbingers of danger. Man has again entered the forest and Bambi must rescue Faline from snarling dogs and escape from a brilliantly animated forest fire. At the end, the cycle of life is renewed. The film does suffer from sentimental and slow moments, but the storytelling is superb and the animation quite fabulous (the direction is credited to David Hand, and the main animators were Frank Thomas, Milt Kahl, Eric Larson and Ollie Johnston). At the time of its release some were even comparing it, incongruously and unfavorably, with the Sabu version of *The Jungle Book* (1942). Nowadays it is more common, and certainly more just, for critics to regard *Bambi* as the last of the really great Disney cartoons.

Cinderella
1950

Roy Disney always used to refer to 1950 as 'our *Cinderella* year.' After a lean period, artistically and financially, *Cinderella* restored morale. It was enthusiastically received and made more money than any Disney film up to that time since *Snow White*.

Charles Perrault's fairy tale has universal appeal and has attracted the attention of such diverse creative talents as Sergei Prokofiev and Jerry Lewis; it was not likely that a fantasist as skilled as Disney would miss his opportunity. It is possible also that this revival of the traditional Disney ingredients – a basic fairy-tale fantasy, a coating of music and magic, an infusion of comedy and charm – came just at the right time. Those children who had warmed to *Snow White* thirteen years before might now have children of their own to introduce to the Disney world.

Ben Sharpsteen supervised the production and the credited directors were Wilfred Jackson, Ham Luske and Clyde Geronimi. Disney was, as usual, constantly on hand with innumerable suggestions on the tiniest details, from the daintiness of the wheels on the fairy carriage to the personality and appearance of the Fairy Godmother. ('It shouldn't be the Deanna Durbin type of thing. I don't see her as goofy or stupid, but rather as having a wonderful sense of humor. Edna May Oliver had sort of what I mean . . .'). Apparently Ward Kimball was having difficulty in coming up with

precisely the right look and feeling for the villainous cat in the tale, Lucifer. After visiting Kimball's home Disney suggested that Kimball's own cat had all the characteristics he needed for the part.

As the leading characters, Cinderella and the prince were treated straight, while the villains, such as the cruel stepmother and vicious stepsisters, were drawn more in the style of caricature. As was often the case in Disney, however, the humans were less interesting or engaging than their animal friends. Lucifer the cat is all feline fearsomeness, though the most sympathetic characters are probably the two comic mice, Jaq and Gus, who are ingeniously voiced by James Macdonald in what has been described as a kind of pidgin, or rodent, Latin. The other main voices are provided by Ilene Woods (Cinderella), William Phipps (Prince Charming) and Verna Felton (Fairy Godmother).

An important ingredient for achieving the right tone and ultimately the success of a Disney film is always the music, and *Cinderella* benefited from an attractive score. 'Bibbidi-Bobbidi-Boo,' written by Mack David, Al Hoffman and Jerry Livingston, was a hit song and nominated for an Oscar; and Oliver Wallace and Paul Smith also secured an Oscar nomination for best scoring of a motion picture. Seen today *Cinderella* lacks the enchantment of vintage Disney; its charm is glassy, overscented somehow. But as Disney's first authentic feature-length fantasy cartoon since *Bambi*, and following years of rather labored product, *Cinderella* glowed for contemporary audiences with the glitter and glory of the fairy castle itself. It was welcomed with open arms.

LEFT: The voice of Cinderella: Ilene Woods.

ABOVE RIGHT: Cinderella on her knees.

RIGHT: The bluebirds are among Cinderella's only friends.

FACING PAGE TOP LEFT: Some of
the retinue of animals that enliven
the action of *Cinderella*.

FACING PAGE TOP RIGHT: The
King and the Duke opposite the
large portrait of the Prince.

LEFT: Cinderella's view of the
glittering fairy castle.

ABOVE: Cinderella's stepmother
and her spiteful stepsisters.

ABOVE RIGHT: The Fairy
Godmother weaves her magic for
Cinderella.

RIGHT: The Fairy Godmother
prepares Cinderella for the ball.

LEFT: The fairy carriage that will take Cinderella to the ball.

BELOW LEFT: The Prince and Cinderella.

RIGHT: The clue of the glass slipper as the search is on for Cinderella.

BELOW RIGHT: Happy ever after: Cinderella weds her Prince Charming.

Alice in Wonderland
1951

Nowadays *Alice in Wonderland* has the reputation of being one of Disney's most intriguing failures. Apparently even Disney himself did not like it very much. The film 'lacks heart,' he said, and it was 'full of weird characters.' This last comment certainly points up the big difference between Disney's personality and that of the author of *Alice*, Lewis Carroll. Carroll is catty more than cute and a sophisticated satirist more than a slapstick sentimentalist. Much of the fun of his writings comes through complicated verbal humor and, although Disney enjoys wordplay in his films, Carroll's is not of a kind that translates easily into visual, cartoon form.

Yet from the outset of his career Disney seems always to have had a desire to put *Alice in Wonderland* in some form on the screen. One of his earliest ventures was the *Alice Comedies* series in 1923, which had nothing to do with Lewis Carroll but did have an actress cavorting in a fantasy world of animated figures. In the early 1930s Disney had seriously proposed doing a version with Mary Pickford as a live-action Alice. However, the project had to be shelved when Paramount brought out their famous 1933 version, co-scripted by Joseph L Mankiewicz and with a stunning cast that included WC Fields as Humpty Dumpty, Cary Grant as the Mock Turtle, Gary Cooper as the White Knight, Edward Everett Horton as the Mad Hatter, and Edna May Oliver as the Queen of Hearts.

The idea surfaced again in the 1940s when Disney commissioned Aldous Huxley to fashion a screenplay partly based on Carroll's stories and partly on episodes in Charles Dodgson's own life. 'I think something rather nice might be made out of this,' wrote Huxley at the time, 'the unutterably odd,

ABOVE: Disney checks the inking of the Alice drawings.

LEFT: Disney discusses the storyboards for *Alice* with Wilfred Jackson.

ABOVE RIGHT: Alice wants to unlock the door to follow the White Rabbit, but she suddenly finds she has shrunk and cannot reach the key on the table.

RIGHT: The encounter with Tweedledum and Tweedledee.

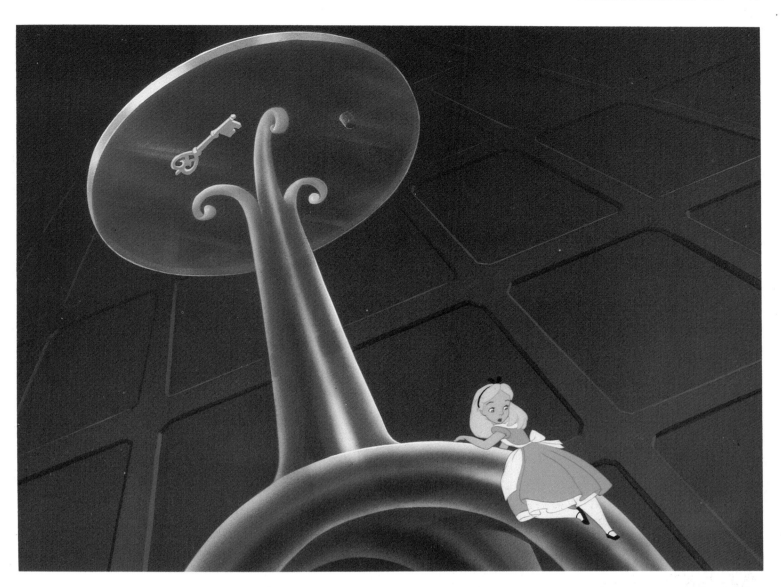

FACING PAGE TOP LEFT: Alice meets the Caterpillar who exhales vowels and riddles – to Alice's great confusion. From *Alice in Wonderland*.

FACING PAGE TOP RIGHT: 'You may have noticed that I'm not all there myself': the Cheshire Cat makes a mysterious appearance – and disappearance.

LEFT: The Mad Hatter and the March Hare at their tea party.

ABOVE: The Queen of Hearts about to play an unusual version of croquet.

ABOVE RIGHT: Alice on trial for causing the Queen to lose her temper. 'Sentence first – verdict afterwards,' declares the Queen.

RIGHT: The Queen's entourage approaches.

LEFT: The characters from Alice's trial (and nightmare) chase her through the maze.

RIGHT: Alice is about to wake from her disturbing dream.

repressed and ridiculous Oxford lecturer on logic and mathematics seeking refuge in the company of little girls and his own fantasy . . .' In a letter Huxley describes a scene he envisaged between Dodgson and Queen Victoria in which Dodgson would, like Lewis Carroll's Alice, exclaim, 'They're nothing but a pack of cards!' and the assembled royalty and distinguished personages would dwindle into cartoon outlines and be scattered to the winds. The ideas sound interesting and Huxley was very enthusiastic, but nothing came of this screenplay. Intriguingly, however, Huxley's concept is similar to that of a film which was released more than forty years later, *Dreamchild* (1985), scripted by Dennis Potter and directed by Gavin Millar. In this film episodes from the life of Dodgson (Ian Holm) are intercut with parallel events from Carroll's fantasy, to produce a beautiful film, with the fantasy creatures superbly created by Jim Henson – a fascinating indicator of the great potential of Huxley's original idea.

However, when Disney's version finally materialized, it was as a traditional feature-length animated film, constricted, Disney thought, not only by having to keep close to Carroll's narrative but also to Tenniel's famous illustrations. Disney's dismay seems to have been shared by his animators and collaborators who, by all accounts, were quite fatigued by the whole enterprise. No fewer than thirteen story men are credited on the film, so it is not surprising that it was widely criticized for being episodic. Ward Kimball, who was largely responsible for some of the best animation in the film (the Cheshire Cat, Tweedledum and Tweedledee, the Mad Hatter's Tea Party), felt that *Alice* suffered from 'too many cooks . . . of one guy trying to top the other guy and make his sequences the biggest and craziest in the show.'

When the film opened the reception was mixed. British critics missed the seductive summer drowsiness of the original and found instead 'cheaply pretty songs' (*The Times*), 'indescribable hullabaloo' (*Observer*) and 'sheer din'

(*Illustrated London News*). It was not simply that Disney had had the gall to omit some much loved characters (the White Knight, the Mock Turtle, Humpty Dumpty). In his desire to popularize Carroll and perhaps temper his occasional savagery, Disney had succeeded in transforming the malice of *Alice* into crude vaudeville.

Yet there are a lot of imaginative strokes in the film. The White Rabbit's song 'I'm Late,' by Sammy Fain and Bob Hilliard, is a superb comedy number. The animation is often brilliant. One thinks of Alice's journey down a rabbit hole that changes color and shape the farther she descends; the weird trees that surround Alice as she looks for the White Rabbit; the startling talking doorknob (a comic detail to which homage will later be paid in *Mickey's Christmas Carol*); the voyage through the Pool of Tears; the March of the Cards; and particularly, the Mad Hatter's Tea Party, which is manically amusing as well as quite mad. Some of the voice characterizations are truly superb, notably Ed Wynn's Mad Hatter, Jerry Colonna's March Hare and Sterling Holloway's Cheshire Cat.

Perhaps the structure is a little too meandering to engage a child's attention all the time, though a similar criticism could be leveled at the original. Perhaps, as Disney thought, Alice is a little too prissy and humorless to gain much sympathy, though again this is a complaint that has often been directed at the story. (Thirty years later the Disney organization's 1985 spectacular *Return to Oz*, which in concept was very similar to *Alice in Wonderland*, would duplicate this fault.) Ultimately the temperaments of Disney and Carroll are probably too far apart, with the result that the mixture comes out as neither vintage Disney nor authentic Carroll. One admires its cleverness, but its situations fail to move one. Yet does that not in a way reveal a truth about Carroll's story? And for those who resist Disneyesque sentiment, is that not a recommendation? Indeed, as the years go by, it is certainly true that Disney's *Alice* gets curiouser and curiouser.

Peter Pan
1953

On the surface, *Peter Pan*, the story of a boy who refuses to grow up, would appear to be ideal Disney territory. Who better than Disney has tapped the child in every adult? And a film would have definite advantages over certain aspects of JM Barrie's play – Peter Pan could be played by a boy, Tinker Bell could become a live creature, and, much more than the stage, a film could really create the illusion of flight. Disney had bought the film rights to Barrie's play in 1939, but getting it onto the screen proved to be problematical.

Coming soon after the failure of *Alice in Wonderland*, *Peter Pan* once again presented Disney with the problem of literary fidelity – he could not upset the purists by tinkering around with the original too much, but would not this have the effect of stifling the imagination of the animators? The directors Hamilton Luske, Clyde Geronimi and Wilfred Jackson had their hands full with problems anyway. Nearly all the characters in the film were humans rather than animals, the only exceptions being Wendy's St Bernard (which behaves like a nanny) and the crocodile (which behaves like Moby Dick). This presented a difficult challenge to the animators, particularly as most of the characterization is quite restrained and naturalistic. Another difficulty was the animation for the flying scenes. How does an animator convey weightlessness?

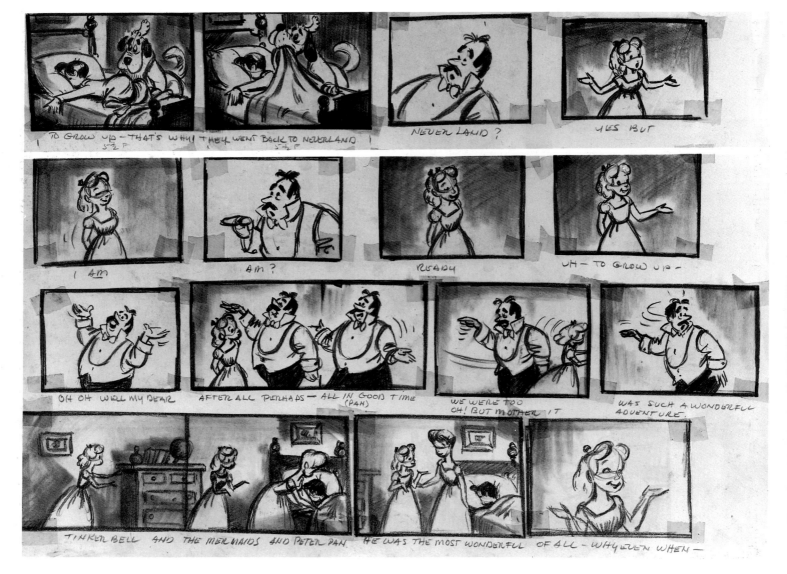

LEFT: A sketch of Tinker Bell.

BELOW LEFT: A storyboard from *Peter Pan* shows Wendy and her parents.

RIGHT: Tinker Bell with her pixie dust.

BELOW: 'You can fly': Peter takes Wendy to Never Land.

As one of the most experienced practitioners, Milt Kahl, said, 'There's nothing harder to do in animation than nothing. *Movement* is our medium.'

The animator Frank Thomas had a particularly hard time with Captain Hook. The reason for this, he said, was a disagreement between the directors and the story editors about the character. Should he be presented as a mean heavy or a foppish dandy? Thomas's final version has elements of both concepts (perhaps more of the latter than the former) and, because he is vocally well played by Hans Conried, Hook is undoubtedly one of the successes of the picture. As always, Disney was full of advice, suggestions and questions. Were Hook's teeth too big? Did the pirate Smee cry too much? Was the tempo right for the fight between Pan and Hook?

In terms of action *Peter Pan* is probably the liveliest cartoon feature from Disney for quite some time. Pan's adventures in Never Land with Wendy and her brothers will involve encounters with pirates, Indians, mermaids, the Lost Boys and a particularly voracious crocodile. Indeed there is so much incident that some of the characters (like the mermaids and the Lost Boys) hardly have an opportunity to establish themselves. Nevertheless the slapstick and the swashbuckling are dispatched with great gusto. The jaws of the crocodile are suitably nightmarish and the humor is engagingly cruel in places (a pirate who is singing 'The Life of a Pirate is Short . . .' is promptly shot in the middle of his refrain). The songs are variable. 'Your Mother and Mine' is a maudlin piece and 'What Made the Red Man Red?' a labored routine, but 'The Second Star to the Right' is an attractive melody, and 'You Can Fly' is certainly one of the classic comedy songs in Disney.

The film has two main themes. The first is established in the opening scene when Wendy's father says she is grown up enough to have a room of her own and that this will be her last night in the nursery, in other words, the last night of her childhood. The adventure with Peter Pan makes it a magical last night, but Wendy recognizes (in the 'Your Mother and Mine' sequence) that the onset of maturity can only be postponed, not stopped. The twinges of incipient adulthood are also foreshadowed through one of the film's subthemes, that of jealousy. Tinker Bell is at first jealous of Wendy, as are the mermaids. Later Wendy will become jealous of the relationship between Peter Pan and the Indian chief's daughter, Tiger Lily. Adolescent sexuality is dawning.

The second theme is the reverse image of the first, and

ABOVE LEFT: Peter Pan lands on the chimney, in search of his shadow.

ABOVE: Magic time: Michael, John, Wendy and Peter.

ABOVE RIGHT: John and the Lost Boys troop off into the jungle.

ABOVE FAR RIGHT: 'What Made the Red Man Red': the Indian dance.

RIGHT: Peter showing the joys of air travel to Wendy and her brothers, John and Michael.

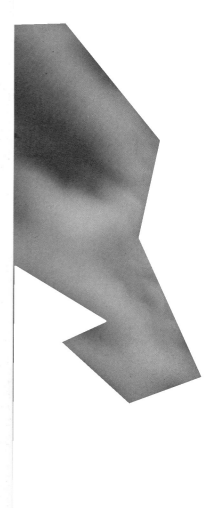

LEFT: 'So you've a taste for cold steel after all!' Captain Hook threatens Peter Pan.

BELOW: Wendy walks the plank.

FAR RIGHT: Peter catches Wendy before she falls into the sea. 'This time you've gone too far, Hook!'

BELOW RIGHT: Peter returns Wendy and her brothers to their London home in the pirate ship, now sprinkled with pixie dust.

equally important. Just as it is inevitable that the child must
grow into adulthood, so is it vital that the adult must not lose
sight of, and contact with, the innocence and wonder of his
childhood. This is confirmed at the end of the film when,
after Wendy has told her parents of her incredible adventure,
her father looks into the night sky and seems to see the
shadow of the ship across the moon. 'You know,' he says, 'I
have the strange feeling I've seen that ship before, long ago,
when I was very young.' He has not lost his childlike vision.

Although the animation does not have the imagination of
Disney at his best, thematically *Peter Pan* expresses funda-
mental and poignant things about Disney's philosophy – the
tension and yet connection between the rival worlds of childhood and adulthood. Its imagery remains memorable and has
surely been an influence on Steven Spielberg. Is not the relationship between Hook and the crocodile remarkably similar
to that between Quint and the shark in *Jaws*? Does not the
image of the shadow of the ship across the moon in *Peter Pan*
anticipate the famous one of the bicycle across the moon in
E.T. (1982)? It should also be remembered that *Peter Pan* has
been mentioned as a possible Spielberg project for years –
and with Dustin Hoffman as Captain Hook.

Lady and the Tramp
1955

Lady and the Tramp, about a love match between a spaniel and a mongrel, is on one level a canine version of *A Place in the Sun* (1951), this time with a happy ending. It also has a lot in common with Billy Wilder's shaggy dog story, *The Emperor Waltz* (1948), which spends a lot of time analyzing, even psychoanalyzing a love affair between a brash American mongrel called Buttons and an aloof Austrian aristocratic poodle by the name of Scheherazade.

Actually the inspiration behind the film dates back to 1937 when Disney was toying with an idea about a suave spaniel and came across a story by Ward Greene about a dog of a much coarser temperament and pedigree. What would happen if the two dogs came together? Disney encouraged Greene to write this up as an idea, and he came up with an opus entitled 'Happy Dan, the Whistling Dog and Miss Patsy, the Beautiful Spaniel.' The project was modified then dropped, then revived, revised and developed, before it finally emerged as *Lady and the Tramp*. Greene and others had reservations about the new title but Disney over-rode their objections – after all, he had thought of it.

Lady and the Tramp was the first Disney cartoon in CinemaScope, which meant it would be difficult for a single character to dominate the frame, so the onus was on the artists to make the backgrounds as interesting as possible. It was also the first of Disney's feature-length cartoons to have a story that nudged its way into the twentieth century, and it therefore demanded a more realistic style. Critics of *Lady and*

LEFT: One of the highlights of *Lady and the Tramp* is a scene in which Peg, a big-hearted Pekingese, sings 'He's a Tramp.'

BELOW: A sketch of the scene when Lady is teased by the Siamese cats.

RIGHT: The dog pound.

BELOW RIGHT: Out of a hatbox jumps the cuddly puppy, Lady.

BELOW FAR RIGHT: Canine curiosity.

ABOVE: Dog about town: the Tramp in *Lady and the Tramp*.

LEFT: Si and Am, two naughty cats who will get Lady into trouble.

ABOVE RIGHT: Malicious feline games, at the expense of a terrified canary and goldfish, and a perplexed Lady.

RIGHT: At Aunt Sarah's insistence, Lady is muzzled.

the Tramp noted that it is a cartoon more dependent on personality than plot, character than comedy.

Lady is a cocker spaniel living contentedly with a married couple whom she knows as 'Jim Dear' and 'Darling.' Her world is complicated when Baby arrives, but the real threat is the arrival of Aunt Sarah and her two mischievous kittens, Si and Am, who proceed to taunt and tease the unfortunate Lady while professing that it is they who are being terrorized. When Lady is taken to a pet shop to be muzzled, she escapes and runs into the mongrel Tramp. From here Lady is to experience the excitement as well as the dangers of freedom, spontaneity and romance.

It is a sentimental film, but also one of some excitement, particularly in a scene where Tramp fights to the death a rat that has been menacing Baby, only to find that he is mistaken as the threat to the child and handed over to the dog catcher. The situation is almost like that of poor Boxer being carried off to the knacker's yard in the film of *Animal Farm* (1954); it also foreshadows the controversial moment in a subsequent Disney film *Old Yeller* when a beloved dog will have to be destroyed. In *Lady and the Tramp*, however, Tramp's friends launch a thrilling attack on the wagon in which he is imprisoned, and the ensuing confusion gives 'Jim Dear' the time to discover the rat behind a drape, realize who the real culprit behind the attack on Baby is, and come to Tramp's aid.

In many ways, though, the most memorable thing about the movie is not the animation but Peggy Lee. She croons 'He's a Tramp . . .' as a soulful blues, punctuated by heartfelt doggy howls; and slinks her way superbly through the song for the Siamese cats who inject a bit of vinegar into the film. The Siamese cat sequence was done by the animator Leo

Salkin who later moved over to UPA. 'Disney was one of the greatest storytellers in and out of the cartoon medium,' Salkin was to say later. 'The difference between Disney's approach and the UPA approach is that the Disney studio is by and large an extension of Walt's thinking whereas UPA allows its directors to work pretty much as *they* see a subject.' *Lady and the Tramp* was only a modest success and it may be that, as Salkin implies, audiences were becoming over-familiar with the Disney style and more aware of possibilities offered by alternative animation, as in UPA's highly successful cartoons like Bob Cannon's *Gerald McBoing Boing* (1951) and Ted Parmelee's *The Tell-Tale Heart* (1953).

ABOVE LEFT: Lady and the Tramp take a stroll.

LEFT: Tramp takes Lady to a back alley behind a restaurant for a delicious meal.

ABOVE: Give me the moonlight: love blossoms on the wrong side of the tracks.

RIGHT: Christmas again – but a new collar for Tramp and a new family for Lady.

Sleeping Beauty
1959

Sleeping Beauty was one of the most elaborate Disney productions of the 1950s. It was six years in the making, involved the skill of three hundred artists, and cost $6 million. It was shot for a wide screen and had full stereo sound for Tchaikovsky's luscious ballet score. It also proved to be one of Disney's biggest failures. When the financial year of 1959-60 proved to be the first time in a decade that the Disney organization had lost money, the explanation was the cost of, and also the lukewarm public response to, *Sleeping Beauty*.

Yet technically the film has much in it to admire. Also the chief villainess, Maleficent, with her blood-red lips, flowing robes and terrifying attendants, is in the grand tradition of Disney malevolence, and is given a fine vocal performance by Eleanor Audley. The film has a striking finale that includes the storming of a Gothic castle; magic that turns boulders into bubbles and cauldrons into rainbows; and a confrontation between the Prince and Maleficent who has now transformed herself into a fire-eating dragon.

Why then did the movie fail to attract much enthusiasm? One reason was that audiences did not seem to have much empathy with the characters. Princess Aurora and Prince Phillip are blandly drawn and look more like two characters out of a 1950s' teen melodrama like *A Summer Place* (1959) than out of a timeless fairy tale. The three Good Fairies, Flora, Fauna and Merryweather are as featureless as their tasteful red, blue and green capes. There is no character in it that a child could love. The absence of emotional warmth might have been emphasized by the wide screen which (as was often the case in the early days of CinemaScope and the other wide-screen processes) not only seemed to slow the pace but to lose the characters in the extra space. Also it was felt at the time that *Sleeping Beauty* looked more like a Disney imitation than a Disney original and, as such, lacked the comparable spell of *Snow White* or *Cinderella*.

The supervising director on the film was Clyde Geronimi, with responsibility for individual sequences being shared by Eric Larson, Wolfgang Reitherman and Les Clark. Disney's instruction to his animators had been to make the characters 'as real as possible, near flesh-and-blood.' This may have been a mistake, for it takes the art of animation too close to that of photography, and fairy tale too close to reality. However, the more usual explanation offered for the film's failure is the absence of Disney himself. When it was put into production, he was so preoccupied with other matters such as the creation of Disneyland and his weekly TV show that he could not give it his close personal supervision. It is an intriguing idea, for a number of Disney employees, before and since, have complained about the boss breathing down their necks, allowing little opportunity for personal expression. If Disney were not there one might have thought that *Sleeping Beauty* offered a liberating freedom from interference. Yet it does not seem to have worked out like that. The technique is as formidable as ever but something – spark, or heart, or perhaps the inimitable Disney touch – is missing.

LEFT: Eyvind Earle devising the stylized backgrounds for one of Disney's most lavish animated features, *Sleeping Beauty*.

ABOVE: A series of four stills to show how live-action film is used by the animator to assist him in his animation – in this case, in his drawing of the horsemanship of Prince Phillip in *Sleeping Beauty*.

RIGHT: The Three Good Fairies: Flora, Fauna and Merryweather.

ABOVE: The mating game: the young lovers are observed by Nature's charming spies, in *Sleeping Beauty*.

LEFT: The Evil Fairy, Maleficent.

RIGHT: A green glow hovers in the castle hallway: the heroine, seemingly hypnotized, follows it.

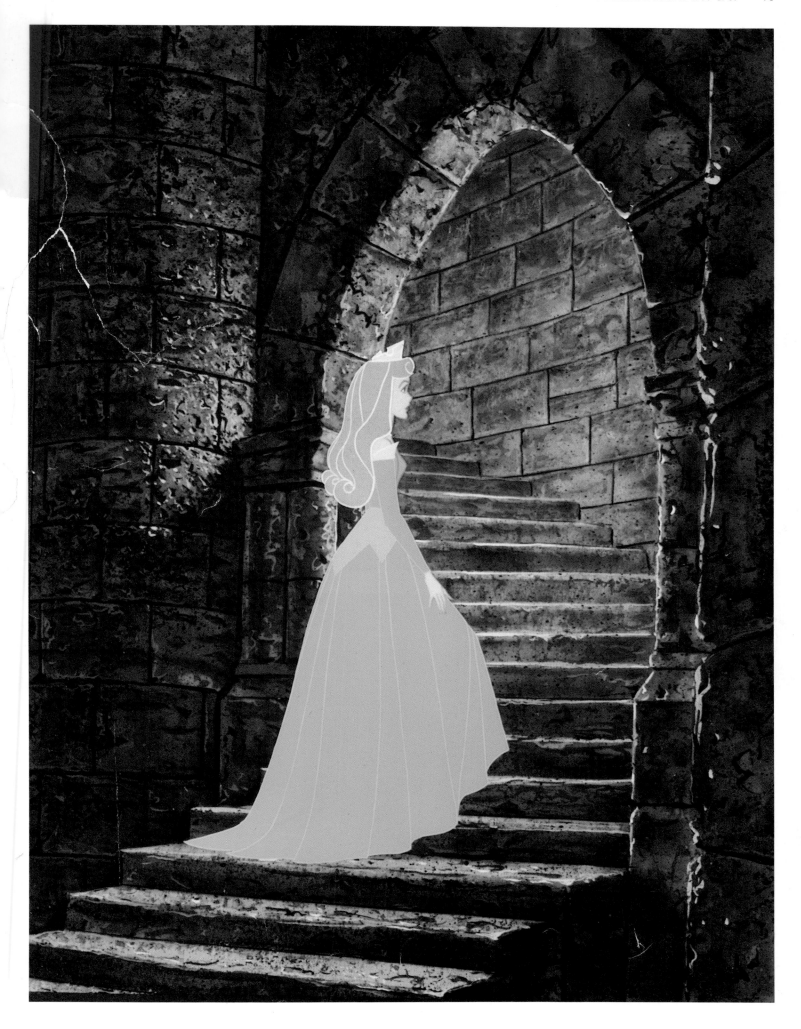

ABOVE: With a kiss, Sleeping Beauty awakens into love.

LEFT: The fiendish Maleficent seems to have the upper hand over the hero.

ABOVE RIGHT: The Good Fairies soaring across the heavens, a good example of *Sleeping Beauty*'s visual spectacle which is sometimes at the expense of exciting character or narrative.

RIGHT: The Prince confronts the Evil Fairy, who has now transformed herself into a fiery dragon.

101 Dalmatians
1961

One of Alfred Hitchcock's golden rules for successful movie-making was: the stronger the villain, the stronger the picture. Disney would support that, with one important modification: the stronger the villain*ess*. Disney's greatest wrongdoers are almost all women and if *101 Dalmatians* is remembered with a shiver of pleasurable affection, the reason is the character of Cruella de Vil, superbly animated by Marc Davis. Mel Leven's song eloquently expounds the depths of her depraved personality: 'If she doesn't scare you, no evil will/To see her is to take a sudden chill . . . /The world was such a wholesome place until . . . /Cruella, Cruella de Vil.'

Based on a novel by Dodie Smith the plot of the film revolves around the theft of numerous Dalmatians. Cruella wants the skins of the dogs for her new overcoats, and to this end employs Horace and Jasper to carry out the theft. However, aided by an old dog, the Colonel, and his Sergeant, a cat called Tibs, the Dalmatians stage a canine mutiny and head back in the ice and snow from Hell Hall where they are being held, toward their home at Regents Park in London. At one stage they have to elude discovery by covering themselves in soot and passing themselves off as Labradors under the nose of the wicked Cruella.

After a soggily sentimental opening about a search for appropriate romantic partners for dog and master, the movie settles down into an exciting chase, with a clear plot and plenty of comedy and suspense. The humor is pleasantly off-beat – a decidedly satirical view of London, after the rather bland re-creation in *Peter Pan*; and some witty jokes about television which include a skittish parody of commercials ('Kanine Krunchies Kommercial') and an ingenious touch of self-congratulation (the Dalmatians' favorite programs are Disney cartoons). While the rest of the film industry was still paranoid about television, Disney was relaxed enough about the cinema's great rival to make jokes about it.

101 Dalmatians also has its innovative touches. Here a Disney feature-length cartoon moves farther than ever before into the twentieth century and Cruella has such an impact perhaps because she seems such a modern figure – a sort of demonic Zsa Zsa Gabor. More significantly, it made use of Ub Iwerks' modification of a Xerox camera to transfer animators' drawings directly onto 'cels' or sheets of celluloid. In the words of the critic Adrian Bailey, this 'allows animators to short-cut traditional techniques and thus preserve the spontaneity of animation sketches.' The old method of hand-inking an animator's pencil drawings would have been impossibly herculean for a movie with 101 main dalmatian characters. Animators would literally have had spots before their eyes, and we would almost certainly have been deprived of one of Disney's most likeable cartoons.

ABOVE: Perhaps Disney's greatest villainess since the Wicked Queen – Cruella de Vil in *101 Dalmatians*.

LEFT: '*Much* too fancy!' Pongo pronounces on dog and owner in *101 Dalmatians*.

RIGHT: Roger and Anita are married, and Pongo and Perdy similarly pledge their fidelity.

LEFT: The puppies are missing, so Pongo decides to try the twilight bark. 'If our puppies are anywhere in the city, the London dogs will know.'

BELOW LEFT: The Colonel confronts the two dognappers, Horace and Jasper.

RIGHT: Captain the horse, Colonel the dog and Sergeant Tibs the cat.

BELOW: Tibs and the Dalmatians are cornered in their bid to escape from Hell Hall.

OVERLEAF: The puppies watch television, particularly their favorite character, Thunderbolt.

LEFT: The Dalmatians escape across a wintry landscape, heading back to London.

BELOW LEFT: Not wanting to be spotted, the Dalmatians are in disguise – but have they deceived Cruella?

RIGHT: 'You're beautiful when you're angry': Cruella gets mad.

BELOW: 'We'll have a Dalmatian plantation,' sings Roger, as he and Anita welcome Pongo, Perdy and the puppies home.

The Sword in the Stone
1963

'The least well-known of Disney's animated films,' comments the Disney historian, Richard Schickel on *The Sword in the Stone*, and Disney's biographer Bob Thomas underlines the point by making not a single reference to it. It is based on T H White's book of the same name and deals with the boyhood of the future King Arthur and his education by the wizard Merlin.

Curiously it was better received in Britain than in America. Whereas American critics attacked it for its thin narrative and its overemphasis on comedy at the expense of awesomeness, British critics liked both its animation and its humor. Part of its interest is its emphasis on three of the most enigmatic yet pervasive characteristics of Disney movies – the obsession with English classics and legends, the characterization of the most evil figures as women (in this case mad Madam Mim), and the recurrent situation of the adopted child who finds sanctuary and fulfillment with a surrogate parent figure.

The film begins reverentially with a shot of T H White's book, the pages turning. A song describes the position of a medieval England without a king and the legend of the sword in the stone ('Whoso pulleth out this sword is rightwise King of England'). 'The strong preyed upon the weak . . .' says the narrator, and by way of illustration a wolf and a hawk are seen closing in on a squirrel. All of these animals are to reappear in different guises later in the film, which is some indication of the film's much criticized but actually quite careful structure. Merlin the Wizard and Archimedes the Owl now appear and, as the smoke from his pipe seems to correspond to the wisps of his imagination, Merlin has a vision of a young boy with a great destiny who will shortly pay a visit. Arthur literally drops in and Merlin undertakes his education.

A number of neat ideas are displayed in this early section. For example, Merlin can see into the future and makes occasional forays into the twentieth century. At the end he will reappear before King Arthur in a becoming pair of Bermuda shorts – he has returned from the twentieth century, he says, 'and, believe me, you can *have* it.' In a prediction of Arthur's future, Merlin says he will become a legend: 'Why – they might even make a motion picture about you.' 'Motion picture?' says Arthur, confused. 'Er – that's something like television, without commercials,' explains Merlin.

There is a lot of amusing detail also in Merlin's lair, notably an automated sugar-bowl that is a bit lavish in its dispensation of sweetness ('When! When!' cries Merlin as it gets out of control. 'Impudent piece of crockery!'). Is this an in-joke about criticisms of Disney's sugary sentimentality? Disney might well have seen a certain similarity between himself and the character of Merlin – both wizards who deal in fantasy and magic and making dreams come true. 'My magic is used mainly for educational purposes,' says Merlin to Arthur's guardian – Disney, as ever, careful to distinguish between good and bad magic.

There is a lot of talk in the film, but Disney and his collaborators (notably the director Wolfgang Reitherman and writer Bill Peet) borrow Hitchcock's gift for making dialogue seem more like part of the atmosphere than detailed exposition. In dialogue terms one scene might be about Arthur's education by Merlin, but visually it is about a big bad wolf trying in vain to gobble up the young boy – the wolf merely succeeds in snapping its mouth shut on its own teeth and sliding down a hill, only to be hit by a rock. The wolf suffers more slapstick indignities than a Blake Edwards hero and is one of the best fall guys in any Disney cartoon.

There are two song sequences, neither of which is particularly relevant but both are delightfully animated. (If the songs have little distinction they do have the virtue of not holding up the action too much.) Having disguised the boy as a fish Merlin now sees him being threatened by a crocodile – educationally the experience is teaching Arthur the lesson of the superiority of brain to brawn. In another disguise, as a red squirrel, Arthur is insistently courted by a red-headed girl squirrel, and even Merlin is pursued by Grandmother Squirrel. All of this provides an excuse for one of those

LEFT: Behind the scenes for *The Sword in the Stone*.

ABOVE RIGHT: The Forest of Wolves.

RIGHT: Educating Arthur: Merlin prepares to teach, while the wolf in hiding prepares for a hearty meal.

tongue-twisting songs beloved by Disney, a bit of gawky romantic humor, and an indication of the limits of Merlin's wizardry. There is no room in Arthur's world for courtship at this point in his life.

The extent of Merlin's magic is fully tested during the film's liveliest section, the encounter with Madam Mim ('who finds a delight in the gruesome and grim'). She stands for the negative potential of magic powers – she touches a rose and it turns black and withers. The magic contest that ensues between her and Merlin is finely done and probably only failed to reap the praise it deserved because a similar comic scene of competing witchcraft had been sparklingly done in a film of roughly the same time, Roger Corman's *The Raven* (1962). The two take on a bewildering change of identities – rabbit, fox, caterpillar, hen, walrus, elephant, mouse, snake, crab, rhino, goat, dragon – and the scene is a riot of color, shape and rhythm. Merlin wins when he become a virus inside Mim. She is last seen languishing on a sickbed moaning 'I hate horrible, wholesome sunshine . . .' For Disney, Mim probably represented the critics.

The Sword in the Stone is perhaps an uneven achievement. Most of the voice characters are excellent, notably Karl Swenson's Merlin and Martha Wentworth's Madam Mim, but some of the dialogue is jarringly anachronistic. 'It's not your fault, I shouldn't have popped off . . .' is the boy's way of apologizing for losing his temper – this sounds more contemporary than medieval Arthurian. Arthur's adopted family is characterized without much personality but Merlin's owl friend, Archimedes (voiced by Junius Matthews), is a typical Disney character, one who hides his good-heartedness under a veneer of grumpiness and is in many ways the film's conscience and its heart. The bumpy plot development toward the end makes the removal of the sword from the stone a bit of an anticlimax, but there are lots of compensations in the superior animation – a stunning panning shot of the images of Arthur and Merlin reflected in a pool as they

walk and converse, and enchanting comic shots of Merlin as a bespectacled fish and of a bullfrog as it swims the backstroke.

The Sword in the Stone strikes one as an unusually thoughtful Disney movie. It shows the co-existence of Good and Evil; for every Merlin there is a Madam Mim, and even when the boy is granted his wish to fly and is transformed into a bird, he must be made aware of the dark side of the dream by being pursued by a hawk. Perhaps the film's contemplative, philosophical tone disappointed those who look to Disney for exhilaration and excitement. For those who come to it without preconceptions it is a stylish entertainment, offering something to think about as well as a feast for the eyes.

LEFT: Merlin, deep in his books. From *The Sword in the Stone*.

ABOVE RIGHT: Merlin returns from the twentieth century ('believe me, you can *have* it') to give King Arthur the benefit of his wisdom.

RIGHT: A young boy has to go through several head-spinning experiences before he can become King of England.

LEFT: The tournament in *The Sword in the Stone*.

ABOVE: 'Whoso pulleth out this sword is rightwise King of England . . .': one of the losers.

RIGHT: The boy lifts the sword from the stone.

The Jungle Book
1967

There is a Muppet joke that runs, 'Do you like Kipling?'/'I don't know – I've never kippled.' Disney's *The Jungle Book* is a cartoon to enchant all those who have never kippled. It is based on Rudyard Kipling's stories about Mowgli, the man-cub adopted by a family of wolves, who grows up in the jungle but whose love for a beautiful Indian girl draws him back toward society. However, unlike the situation with *Alice in Wonderland* and *Peter Pan*, Disney seems not to have been intimidated by his prestigious literary source. 'Here's the original by Rudyard Kipling,' he said to writer Larry Clemmons. 'The first thing I want you to do is not to read it.'

During the making of the movie there was some concern that there might not be a strong enough storyline. The gags were good, but the structure looked loose. By all accounts, however, Disney himself remained serenely confident. He felt the characterization was strong and would therefore carry it through, and he was right.

Three things in particular contributed to the film's success, two of which were expected and traditional, one of which was unconventional and controversial. Firstly, Mowgli, Bagheera the panther, Baloo the bear, Shere Khan the tiger, the elephants and the apes were all expertly animated, and the snake was superb. Secondly, *Jungle Book* had the strongest score of any Disney feature cartoon for a long time, arguably since *Dumbo*. Terry Gilkyson's song 'The Bare Necessities' was nominated for an Oscar for best song, amazingly losing out to a tuneless ditty from *Dr Doolittle* (1967) whose title would fit Disney's film as well as its own: 'If I Could Talk to the Animals.' The musical highlight of *The Jungle Book*, however, is probably the Richard and Robert Sherman number, 'I Wanna Be Like You,' in which a groovy Baloo the Bear ('I'm gone, man – solid gone') joins in the fun with the king of the apes in one of the most celebrated musical routines in postwar Disney. The songs are in the modern style – there was no real attempt anywhere to evoke the period of the story – but are so good that no one minded.

The third element in the successful brew proved, in retrospect, to be the most contentious. It was decided to give the film a new range of voices for the cartoon characters by using stars. This was not done right through the cast. The indestructible, indispensable Sterling Holloway did the snake, and Mowgli was rather weakly done in the voice of an American child (the rather whining voice performances of children in Disney cartoons is frequently a weakness). However, the most vivid cartoon characters were, as it were, put into the mouths of well-loved, easily recognizable entertainers – the suavely sinister George Sanders as the tiger, the bouncy Louis Prima as the ape, and the unmistakably cuddly tones of Phil Harris as the bear. Disney himself had suggested Harris for the role.

There is no doubt that this fresh vocal coloring had a powerful impact on the film. Inevitably it had an impact on the animation, for the animators would be tempted, indeed encouraged, to incorporate familiar characteristics of the performing personalities into the cartoon characters they played. 'It is much simpler and more realistic,' said director Wolfgang Reitherman, 'than creating a character and then searching for the right voice.' However, some Disney aficionados were dismayed by this development, feeling that it amounted to laziness of imagination. As the critic Leonard Maltin asked: are we identifying with the characters, or with the stars who provide the voices? And, to extend that idea further, is not the vocal personality of Phil Harris so strong and distinctive that the characters he will play for Disney – Baloo the bear in *The Jungle Book*, Thomas O'Malley cat in *The Aristocats* (1970), Little John in *Robin Hood* (1973) – will essentially become the same character?

It should be said that the vast majority of audiences seem not to have been as bothered by this as some critics. Many find *The Jungle Book* the most purely delightful Disney film since *Dumbo* and it was still taking sizeable sums at the box-office when it was reissued in 1984. Perhaps the beginning is slow and the ending sentimental but most of it works like a charm. For first audiences of the film the delight was tinged with sadness, as Disney died before it was released. He could not have wished for a finer memorial.

LEFT: A cat nap: Mowgli with his friend, Bagheera the panther.

ABOVE: Kaa the snake at his most mesmerizing, superbly hissed by Sterling Holloway.

RIGHT: Close encounter: Mowgli and the elephant.

OVERLEAF: Trunk call.

LEFT: Mowgli and the jungle VIP – the ape-king of the swingers.

ABOVE: Baloo the bear, voiced by Phil Harris who had been chosen for the role by Disney, dances with Mowgli.

RIGHT: The only way to travel.

LEFT: In *The Jungle Book* the fearsome Shere Khan the tiger menaces Mowgli throughout the film.

ABOVE: Cackling birds: cousins of the crows in *Dumbo*?

RIGHT: Mowgli on the path of true love.

From Animation to Actors

Live-Action and Documentary Films 1948-1967

There is a story that, when President Sukarno of Indonesia visited Disneyland shortly after its opening in 1955, he was so overwhelmed by the lavish spectacle that he turned to Disney and said, 'Mr Disney, you must be a very wealthy man.' 'Yes, I guess I am,' replied Disney, then added 'they tell me I owe about $10 million.'

Until the 1950s the finances of the Disney operation were always quite precarious, with Walt continually exhausted from the strain, as he put it, of having to live from picture to picture. There is no doubt that his diversification into documentary and live-action features was partly determined by economic considerations such as lower outlay, less risk and faster return on investment. The question is: at what *aesthetic* cost? Is the eminent film historian David Shipman right when he brutally opines that the richer Disney became, the worse his films became?

Whereas in the 1930s it was commonplace to see Disney mentioned in the same breath as Capra and Chaplin as one of the authentic artists of the American screen, it is possible, even conventional, to read a history of Hollywood achievement in the 1950s without finding a single reference to Disney. Whereas Alfred Hitchcock's increasing celebrity in the 1950s through television coincided with a growing complexity and mastery of his film art, Disney's increasing television celebrity ran alongside what most critics felt was a disappointing decline in artistic stature, and they agonized over the reasons for it. Had he sold out to commercialism?

Were other preoccupations – notably television and Disneyland – getting in the way of his usual close supervision of his product? Had he been intimidated by the new generation of animators working for production companies like UPA, whose cartoons revealed a much darker, more iconoclastic spirit than the modern Disney?

Disney could afford to ignore the critics because there were two factions of the film audience that kept faith with him during this time – the industry and the general public. His True-Life Adventure series of nature films might have antagonized the purists, as we shall see, but they thrilled the public, won awards and pioneered a new form – the general-interest nature film or what one could even call the *entertaining* documentary. Although hardly any of Disney's live-action feature films during his lifetime rate much more than a footnote in most film histories of the period they generally passed the time pleasantly, gently inculcated traditional values and wrung the occasional tear out of the stock situation of the separation of child from parent. This formula of modest family film fare also made money and continued to do so until the mid-1970s.

The feature films fall into several clear categories. There are the swashbuckling adventures, with heroes like Robin Hood or Dick Turpin; or the adaptations of children's classics, such as *Swiss Family Robinson* (1960); or the respectful versions of famous authors, like Robert Louis Stevenson (*Treasure Island*, 1950; *Kidnapped*, 1960) or Jules Verne

LEFT: Fred MacMurray as Professor Ned Brainard and his dog Charlie in *The Absent Minded Professor*. The Professor has just discovered 'flubber.'

RIGHT: The marauding pirates in *Swiss Family Robinson* (1960).

(*20,000 Leagues Under the Sea*, 1954; *In Search of the Casta-ways*, 1962). There are also westerns like *Davy Crockett* (1955), old-fashioned and conventional in characterization and outlook during one of the most questioning and dynamic eras in the genre's history. Finally there are the whimsical comedies, invariably with a dash of an extra ingredient – sentiment (*Pollyanna*, 1960), music (*The Happiest Millionaire*, 1967) or animals (*That Darn Cat*, 1965). If the gimmick is more important than the characters (as in *Moon Pilot*, 1962; or *The Gnome-Mobile*, 1967), then there will be no stars but low-key romantic leads like Dean Jones or Suzanne Pleshette and reliable character actors like Brian Keith or Ed Wynn.

Disney's feature films are rarely generous with star names. Hayley Mills and Fred MacMurray were Disney's most regular star employees and they were never blockbuster names in themselves. Fess Parker was Disney's symbol of American manhood but he never emerged as anything more than a marked-down John Wayne. James MacArthur was Disney's James Dean – without the neurosis, of course, but also without the charisma. Interestingly he extended this policy to directors, rarely employing anyone with even a semblance of a distinctive personality or style of his own. The absence of star names or ambitiously creative directors probably served the dual purpose of keeping costs down and ensuring that Disney's own name was the star attraction – which was fair enough since audiences were undoubtedly attracted mainly because of the Disney trademark.

· In live-action feature films the Disney trademark stood for something considerably more cautious, less innovative – technically and thematically – than the cartoons. It is curious that, as a filmmaker, Disney always seemed more at home

LEFT: Fred MacMurray plays the scoutmaster in the sentimental *Follow Me Boys* (1966), a movie which, as *Monthly Film Bulletin* said, 'demands an extremely strong stomach.'

BELOW LEFT: Based on a novel by Jules Verne, *In Search of the Castaways* stars Hayley Mills (left) as a girl searching for her missing father.

BELOW RIGHT: A boy's best friend: *Old Yeller* (1957).

RIGHT: A brave group of Irish rebels mount a surprise attack on their English oppressors in *The Fighting Prince of Donegal* (1966).

with drawings than with people, and could make them seem more human. He never dealt with adult relationships in these films, nor ever seemed to want to, and he never made a live-action feature with even a modicum of contemporary social comment (which might be why they were so successful, of course: audiences responded to their pure escapism). Probably the nearest he got to realism was his insistence in *Old Yeller* (1957) that the boy shoot his beloved dog after it had been bitten by a rabid wolf. But this is not really a nod in the direction of screen realism; rather, it is Disney simply being ecologically sensible.

By the mid-1960s the patience of some commentators was exhausted. Pauline Kael and Judith Crist weighed in with anti-Disney diatribes. For Pauline Kael the breaking-point was *The Ugly Dachshund* (1966), a sort of four-legged version of *Pollyanna*. Ms Kael walked out halfway through, railing against Disney's reduction of childhood wonder to cuteness and sentimentality, and speculating about whatever happened to good adventure movies that were enjoyable to both adults and children. For Judith Crist the crunch came with *Follow Me Boys* (1966), an extended hymn to Fred Mac-Murray's saintly scoutmaster which Ms Crist described as 'one of the worst films ever to emanate from the Disney

studios, a near-parody of all the low-brow small-townery that has given Disney's features a bad name among intellectuals who never go to Disney movies.'

Although Disney would have scorned the reference to 'intellectuals' ('urban hicks' was his term for them), he was periodically irritated by this kind of vituperation. Could his films be that bad if the public continued to pay to see them? Admittedly not all of them attracted the public. Who now remembers *Toby Tyler* (1960), *Third Man on the Mountain* (1959) or *The Fighting Prince of Donegal* (1966)? Would anyone recall *Darby O'Gill and the Little People* (1959) if it did not contain a collector's gem – the sight and sound of a young Sean Connery bursting into song? Yet there are some good films tucked away amid the cotton candy. *20,000 Leagues Under The Sea* (1954) endures as a fine adventure; *The Absent Minded Professor* (1961) still stands up as inventively surrealist film comedy; and, of course, there is *Mary Poppins* (1964). As that rogue Flashman used to say, never kick a man when he's down – he may get up. *Mary Poppins* was the most successful film to be released during Disney's lifetime and critically the best received since *Snow White*. Just when it was thought he had lost the knack, the Merlin of the movies showed he still possessed the magic touch.

Seal Island
1948

One of Disney's greatest admirers during the 1930s was the critic and filmmaker Pare Lorentz, who is best remembered for two classics of American documentary film, *The Plow That Broke the Plains* (1936) and *The River* (1937). It is possible that this admiration was reciprocated when Disney himself decided to branch into documentary. Although Disney's documentaries have none of the social commitment of Lorentz's films, they do have in common an underlying ecological theme, a fascination with various aspects of Americana and an essentially lyrical rather than polemical approach to the documentary form.

Disney's venture into his famous nature film series of True-Life Adventures began with *Seal Island*. This derived initially from his interest in Alaska and his exploration of the possibilities of making a movie about Alaskan life. To this end he had approached Al and Elma Milotte, owners of a camera store in Alaska, who had earned a high reputation as movie photographers through the informational shorts they had made for industry and the military. Disney invited them to shoot material on any aspect of Alaskan life which seemed to them interesting or different, and eventually they proposed a film about the seals which migrated annually to the Pribilof Islands to mate and raise their pups.

The Milottes spent a year living with the Eskimos, shooting miles of film which was eventually edited down to 27 minutes. The life cycle of the seals imposed a basic narrative structure on the material, which elsewhere was periodically enlivened by a playful bit of montage and music (a fight edited rhythmically to the music of Verdi's 'Anvil Chorus' from *Il Trovatore*, for example). Musical manipulation of this kind was to become something of a feature in Disney's documentaries – and one of the most controversial ones.

ABOVE: Seal pups: their first swimming lesson?

LEFT: Sealed with a kiss.

RIGHT: A sea of seals.

LEFT: Seal pups get their marching orders in *Seal Island*.

BELOW LEFT: The poster for *Seal Island*, advertising it as a 'True Life Adventure' and referring to its Academy Award-winning success.

BELOW RIGHT: The cast and crew from *Treasure Island*.

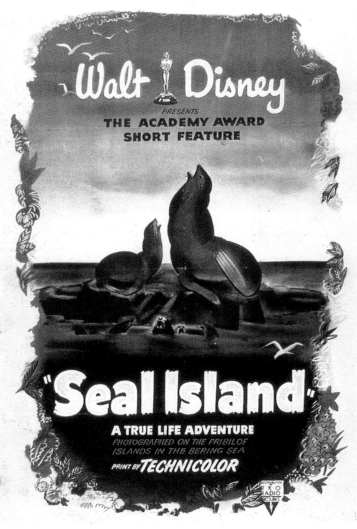

'Who wants to look at seals playing on a bare rock?' This was the attitude Disney encountered from most exhibitors, who saw no commercial potential in a film that was essentially a nature documentary. Even brother Roy opposed the idea of the nature films, fearing they might prove expensive and esoteric. Opposition to his obduracy invariably made Disney more determined than ever to prove that the doubters were wrong. Walt booked *Seal Island* into a theater in Pasadena in time for it to qualify for consideration for the Academy Awards, and it was not only nominated for but subsequently won the Oscar as the best two-reel short film of 1948. Legend has it that the morning after the Oscar presentation Walt marched into his brother's office and told him to go knock RKO over the head with it.

Seal Island was the first of a number of short films about nature that Disney was to produce in the next few years. They turned out to be relatively cheap to shoot. Although they did not make an enormous amount of money from the projects, the photographers who were assigned were generally happy, for they were working on subjects quite different from the average and their equipment was far superior. Most important of all for the nature photographer, a generous amount of time was allotted. Stories about the painstaking photography on a Disney documentary are legion – six weeks to film the hatching of an alligator's egg, for example, or forty days to get a close shot of a heron catching a fish. Of the subsequent films, *In Beaver Valley* (1950) and *Bear Country* (1953) were among the most popular. Other subjects chosen included elks, water birds and the evocatively titled *Prowlers of the Everglades*. They fulfilled ideally Disney's dual concept of his role in the film industry – not only as entertainer now but as educator too. As had happened with the cartoons, it was inevitable that the format would be expanded to feature length.

Treasure Island
1950

In 1949 Disney had made a film about life on a country farm at the turn of the century, *So Dear to My Heart*. The subject was probably dear to Disney's heart, reminding him of his childhood, but the film is less interesting for its content than for its form. Although the film has a few sequences of animation, it was mainly a conventional live-action feature, starring Beulah Bondi, Burl Ives and the child actor Bobby Driscoll. It was clear that Disney was ready to diversify into undiluted live-action features, and the first, and one of the best, was *Treasure Island*.

It was appropriately made in England, with funds that had been frozen during the Second World War and could only be spent in England. This no doubt influenced the choice of subject as well as Disney's decision to make a series of adventure films in England that were generally modest, straightforward pictorializations of familiar legends or children's classics. Yet Disney's career, as we shall see, reveals a mysterious fascination for things British, notably works that were either published or are set in the Victorian or early Edwardian period.

Robert Louis Stevenson's classic novel of piracy, stolen maps and hidden treasure had been published in 1883 and already filmed twice – in 1918 by Maurice Tourneur, with the novelty of a female (Shirley Mason) in the role of the boy Jim Hawkins who falls into the hands of Long John Silver and his scurvy cut-throats; and in 1934 by Victor Fleming, with Wallace Beery and young Jackie Cooper in the leading roles. Disney ensured that the new version stuck quite closely to the outline of the novel and, apparently to ensure the clarity of the narrative and the interest of the characters, he insisted that it should be storyboarded in as much detail as his cartoons. The characterizations certainly do come through and the situation of Hawkins – an isolated child in search of a father figure he can trust and cherish – is the kind of disrupted family situation one often finds in Disney's films, all the way from *Pinocchio* (1940) to *Something Wicked This Way Comes* (1983).

An efficient professional, Byron Haskin, was assigned to direct – he is now best remembered for his direction of the Martians in *The War of the Worlds* (1952) and the ants in *The Naked Jungle* (1954) – and the photography was entrusted to Freddie Young, later to be renowned for his magnificent camera-work on three David Lean epics, *Lawrence of Arabia* (1962), *Dr Zhivago* (1965) and *Ryan's Daughter* (1970). Bobby Driscoll was cast in the role of Hawkins, which led to some quibbles about the casting of a young American in this quintessentially English role. But as the critic of the *Observer*, C A Lejeune, eruditely pointed out, there was nothing incongruous about casting an American in that role, since the novel was actually dedicated to a young American – Lloyd Osborne, Stevenson's future stepson – as being the kind of adventure he would like. In fact, as his performance in the thriller *The Window* (1949) demonstrated, Driscoll was at that time probably the best child actor around.

LEFT: Bobby Driscoll played Jim Hawkins and Robert Newton played Long John Silver in *Treasure Island*.

RIGHT: The pirates approach the island in *Treasure Island*.

BELOW: Jim finds the pirate treasure at last.

However, one does not remember this *Treasure Island* for its Jim Hawkins, but for its quite unforgettable Long John Silver. Robert Newton's performance – replete with wooden leg, mad grin, rolling cadences and the most agitated eyeballs since Eddie Cantor's – caught the imagination of the public and the breath of the critics. It was a performance that seemed closer to popular pantomime than to adventure classic, and the critics found its bold, outrageous melodrama more appropriate to a cartoon rogue than a human being. 'He is as sweet as a spoonful of sugar held high over the porridge plate,' said the critic Paul Holt, 'as tricky as an ageing jockey, as succulent as peach-fed ham.' Everyone was certainly struck by the ham, and opinions continue to be divided over whether his performance was priceless or preposterous.

More generally the film was well received. Perhaps it was solid more than imaginative and lacked the danger and tension of the original; perhaps it had the air of a festive party rather than a perilous adventure; and perhaps, as Dilys Powell said, it was still true that Disney 'can make us care far more about the fortunes of a painted duck, mouse, dog or elephant than the fate of all these honest chaps in search of pirate gold.' Nevertheless, as an unpretentious entertainment that would appeal to all ages, the movie was an unqualified success, critically and commercially.

What was Disney's own response to this experience of working with actors? Alfred Hitchcock had once made an amusing remark about Disney's advantage over him when it came to casting: 'If he doesn't like someone, he just tears him up.' Yet Disney was now reveling in some of the compensations of working with humans, and during the making of *Treasure Island* he would playfully needle his animators. 'These actors in England are great,' he would say. 'You give 'em the lines, they rehearse a couple of times, and you've got it on film – it's finished. You guys take six months to draw a scene.' Behind the jocular jibe, one can sense a serious commercial consideration being turned over in Disney's mind. It was not simply that feature-film production was a mode of operation that had the appeal of novelty for Disney. Clearly production on this modest scale was likely to prove more profitable and certainly less risky than a full-length cartoon. The critical and commercial failure first of *Alice in Wonderland* and then later *The Sleeping Beauty* would only serve to accelerate these thoughts and so confirm Disney's new commitment to live-action features.

The Story of Robin Hood
1952

Nobody would make great claims for the imaginative cinematic qualities of the films Disney made in Britain in the 1950s. Yet they succeeded in what they set out to do – entertain, and make a profit. They were probably shrewdly timed. *The Story of Robin Hood*, *Rob Roy* (1953) and *The Sword and the Rose* (1953) all had royalist themes which were undoubtedly welcome to a British public in the throes, and then aftermath, of Coronation fever, following the Coronation of Queen Elizabeth II on 2 June 1953.

Part of the appeal of the films was probably the way they also succeeded in conveying a good-natured team spirit. Although the personnel were not identical in this trio of films, there was sufficient cross-over in cast and technicians to give them a unity of appearance. The cast included Richard Todd to embody noble heroism, Glynis Johns for capricious femininity, James Robertson Justice for amiable bluster and Michael Gough for suave duplicity.

The Story of Robin Hood and His Merrie Men (to give it its full title) certainly pales in comparison with earlier film versions of the legend starring Fairbanks and Flynn. But Disney had a different audience in mind and his film is like an illustrated children's picture-book. The story rings a few changes from tradition. Here Robin is a forester's son, Robert Fitzooth (Richard Todd), who becomes the outlaw Robin Hood after his father has been murdered by mercenaries of the evil Sheriff of Nottingham (Peter Finch, of all people). Gathering support in Sherwood Forest, Robin and his men wage guerrilla warfare against the sheriff and Prince John (Hubert Gregg), who has instituted a reign of terror during King Richard's absence on the Crusades. The main spectacle is an archery contest and a fight to the death between Robin and the sheriff, and predictably Robin is eventually pardoned by King Richard. Joan Rice plays a spunky Maid Marian, James Robertson Justice a hefty Little John, while Elton Hayes as the balladeer Alan-a-Dale punctuates the action with songs designed to lift fact into legend. The film itself, self-effacingly directed by Ken Annakin, is resolutely prosaic but still pleasant.

ABOVE: Joan Rice plays the tomboyish Maid Marian, opposite Richard Todd's Robin Hood.

RIGHT: Richard Todd (left) as Robin Hood and James Hayter (right) as Friar Tuck.

ABOVE RIGHT: 'Stand aside and let the better man pass!': Robin Hood (Richard Todd, right) has his first encounter with Little John (James Robertson Justice).

LEFT: Target practice for Robin Hood (Richard Todd, right) is made complicated when Maid Marian (Joan Rice, left) keeps moving the target.

The Sword and the Rose
1953

If *Rob Roy* is the most exciting of Disney's royalist trilogy, *The Sword and the Rose* is probably the most elaborate. The plot concerns King Henry VIII's attempt to pull off a political marriage between his sister Mary (Glynis Johns) and the ailing King of France, Louis XII, a ruse that is complicated when Mary falls for an English commoner, Brandon (Richard Todd). Michael Gough is on hand again to provide his polished display of oily English Machiavellianism.

The problem with the film is its lack of narrative energy. (The direction is again by Ken Annakin, a favorite British director of Disney, who would also make *Swiss Family Robinson* for him.) The first half-hour is little more than a guided tour of Tudor lifestyle. Lawrence Watkin's screenplay is full of attempted period exclamations like 'Cover yourself, hussy!' and ''Tis a wench!,' not to mention incongruous verbal felicities such as Mary's instruction to Brandon to 'gather a nosegay and compose me a sonnet,' or a lady-in-waiting's plaintive query, 'Would you put his neck in jeopardy for the sake of a springtime dalliance?' Still, there is an invigorating dosage of mischievous comedy as Mary cunningly attempts to hasten the demise of her frail French husband; and just occasionally there are flickerings of thoughtful themes – the responsibilities of royalty, and the role of women in a male-dominated society.

The role of the hero is uncomplicated and the same in all three films – one that reconciles rebelliousness with royalist loyalty. 'You are a great rogue,' says the king to Rob Roy, who replies with studied sincerity: 'You are a great king.' Richard Todd is hardly the most dashing of screen actors, but the three heroes he plays are people with whom Disney would have great empathy: individualists, pioneers, thorns in the side of the conventional establishment but, at heart, traditional nationalists. Robin Hood, Rob Roy and Brandon are all misunderstood patriots for whom things will eventually go their way. No wonder Disney understood them. The movies also reveal Disney's passion for the English past which was to culminate in his loving re-creation of Edwardian London in *Mary Poppins*.

ABOVE: Brandon (Richard Todd, left) impresses Mary (Glynis Johns, right) with some fancy footwork in *The Sword and the Rose*.

RIGHT: Mary (Glynis Johns, left) tries to soothe her sulky and volatile brother Henry VIII (James Robertson Justice, right).

LEFT: The villainous Michael Gough (right) is cornered by Richard Todd (left) while Glynis Johns (center) watches anxiously. From *The Sword and the Rose*..

The Living Desert
1953

Disney's first full-length nature film, *The Living Desert*, was inspired by a ten-minute film made by Paul Kenworthy in which he had photographed a deadly duel between a wasp and a tarantula. Disney thought that this kind of dramatic observation of nature in action could be elaborated at feature length. As was the custom for a Disney nature documentary, a team of photographers was given the theme and then sent on location to find and film the raw material. When sent back, it was edited into shape under the general supervision of James Algar, Ben Sharpsteen and Winston Hibler.

The photography of *The Living Desert* was spectacular and put together with great flair. It had an eye for both the poetry and violence of animal life, and the grandeur of the natural settings. Time-lapse photography was used to show the process of a flower coming into full bloom. A scene of high drama was created from the rise and surge of floodwater across the wilderness and the slow but sure process whereby it is sucked into the desert sands. The violent encounter between wasp and tarantula was now enlarged to include other combatants – snake versus rat, hawk versus rattlesnake. Disney was active in giving advice on how these events should be interpreted, and the tone he wanted from the narration and the music. The wasp/tarantula struggle, for example, was not there simply to be observed as a fact of nature: the participants should be characterized and the struggle portrayed as a study in skill versus strength.

Unexpectedly, films like *The Living Desert* turned out to be among the most controversial Disney ever made. There had been mutterings for years about anthropomorphism in Disney cartoons, and the documentaries intensified the debate. 'Any time we saw an animal doing something with style or personality,' said a Disney writer, 'we capitalized on

it. But they say we're putting people into animal suits.' Actually, in *The Vanishing Prairie* (1954) a cameraman literally donned an animal suit so that he could mingle with a buffalo herd. By all accounts the buffaloes (unlike the critics) did not seem to mind.

Perhaps the scene that caused most contention in *The Living Desert* was the filming of the mating ritual of two scorpions, re-edited and presented, through the music and the narration, in the manner of a square dance. It was typical of Disney to inject a dash of comedy into the usual dour dryness of documentary features. For a critic like Gordon Gow it was a 'technically stunning little sequence.' Others felt it was a

ABOVE: Guess who's coming to dinner: the struggle for survival in *The Living Desert*.

LEFT: A flower comes into full bloom.

RIGHT: Hitching a lift in *The Living Desert*.

ABOVE: A hawk swoops down to attack a rattlesnake, one of the scenes that had squeamish critics complaining of *The Living Desert*'s 'excessive violence.'

LEFT: Hands full: Disney clutching his four Oscars at the 1954 Academy Award ceremony: for *The Living Desert* (best documentary feature), *Bear Country* (best two-reel short), *The Alaskan Eskimo* (best documentary short), and *Toot, Whistle, Plunk and Boom* (best short cartoon).

TOP RIGHT: Buffalo skins were used to disguise the presence of cameramen shooting *The Vanishing Prairie*, so they could move freely among the herd.

ABOVE RIGHT: Shuffle off to buffalo: a buffalo family in *The Vanishing Prairie*. For Disney, the buffalo symbolized America's pioneering past.

what Bosley Crowther called its 'zoological morbidity.' Certainly the emphasis on eat-or-be-eaten recalls Woody Allen's comparison of nature to an 'enormous restaurant' in his film *Love and Death* (1975).

Disney might have been hurt by these criticisms, but most accounts suggest he was mainly baffled by them. He could not see their relevance. The documentary was there of course for information and wonder, but what was wrong in bringing to it a bit of entertainment and emotion? His approach to the documentary was not that of a natural scientist or objective observer and analyst, but that of an entertainer and storyteller who knew how to grab the attention and touch the feelings of his audience. He was after cinematic impact above all, and once again his instincts were vindicated. The film won an Oscar for best documentary and was a huge hit with the general public.

As a footnote it should be noted that *The Living Desert* led to a break between Disney and his longtime distribution partner, RKO. The indifference of RKO to the film persuaded Walt and Roy to set up their own distribution subsidiary which they called Buena Vista after the street on which the Disney Studio was situated. This new arrangement cut distribution costs and, crucially, gave them control over the packaging and timing of a film's release. The launch of *The Living Desert*, supported on their program by a fine cartoon, *Ben and Me*, was very successful and a sign of things to come in the care Buena Vista put into packaging a program of Disney product in the most advantageous way possible.

travesty. After all, they complained, it is amazing enough that scorpions mate at all: why jazz it up? 'The playful disposition to edit and arrange,' said Bosley Crowther, 'so that it appears the wildlife is behaving in human and civilized ways is not true to life.' The British documentarian, Basil Wright, was even more harsh. 'The equation of Mickey Mouse or Donald Duck with humans is justified by the fact that nothing is real,' he argued. But 'animals and birds and insects *are* real, and are not fair game for wisecracks . . . it is like putting elephants in pinafores. The result is that it is we, not they, who are being made fools of.'

There were also complaints from the critics about what they thought was the patronizing tone of the narration and the music, and even some objections to the film's violence –

20,000 Leagues Under the Sea
1954

One of the secrets of Disney's success was that he never rested on his laurels. A year rarely went by when he was not trying out something different and innovative in one of his films. In the case of his film adaptation of Jules Verne's nineteenth-century classic *20,000 Leagues Under the Sea* there were several unusual features. It was the first Disney feature in CinemaScope and indeed the first science-fiction movie in CinemaScope. (Most sci-fi film historians give credit to Disney's film for elevating the status of the sci-fi movie, until then usually low-budget and shot in black and white.) Also unusual was the fact that the film had a cast that was starry enough (Kirk Douglas, James Mason, Paul Lukas, Peter Lorre) to rival Disney himself for top billing. Finally, the budget was large – $5 million, $250,000 of which was spent on the creation of a giant squid whose attack on the crew members would be the action highlight of the film.

Investigating the mysterious disappearance of sailing vessels in the South Pacific, a ship is capsized by what looks to be a gigantic sea monster. However, when three survivors, a marine biologist (Paul Lukas), his assistant (Peter Lorre) and a harpoonist (Kirk Douglas) are captured, it turns out that the monster is actually a futuristic submarine, the *Nautilus*, run by the embittered megalomaniac, Captain Nemo (James Mason). The biologist is awed by this civilization beneath the sea (superbly evoked in an Oscar-winning design by John Meehan), but the harpoonist's only desire is to escape. Many adventures will ensue before this desire is satisfied and Nemo's world is destroyed.

The film's direction was entrusted to the capable hands of Richard Fleischer, who at that time had made a speciality of directing high-class thrillers like *The Narrow Margin* (1952) and who in retrospect is probably the best feature-film director Walt Disney ever worked with. There was just one ticklish point to negotiate – Fleischer was the son of one of Disney's arch animation rivals, Max Fleischer, creator of Popeye. However, Fleischer sought the approval of his father and it was duly given.

The shooting of the film was complicated but very efficiently dispatched. Some of the action was shot in a studio tank but a lot on location in the Bahamas, which Fleischer found ideal because of 'its picturesque coral formations, its abundance of fish life, and its crystal-clear water.' Disney's instruction to Fleischer was typical: 'Show the audience what it is like to be underwater. Make it believable, make it real.' After making the film, Fleischer was to claim it contained more underwater footage than any previous motion picture, and that one scene of an underwater burial – a moment that first attracts the attention of the survivors to their strange new world – required forty people to be present at the ocean's depths, twenty in front of the camera, twenty behind.

Such striving for authenticity would not count had the characterization not come to life. The strong cast is excellent.

LEFT: Building the giant squid for *20,000 Leagues Under the Sea*.

ABOVE: The submarine *Nautilus* on the ocean bed.

RIGHT: Head-hunters attacking the *Nautilus* leap from its electrified deck in this scene from Walt Disney's *20,000 Leagues Under the Sea*, starring Kirk Douglas, James Mason, Paul Lukas and Peter Lorre.

ABOVE: The battle with the giant squid in *20,000 Leagues Under the Sea*.

LEFT: Native boatmen.

ABOVE RIGHT: The poster for *20,000 Leagues Under the Sea*.

FAR RIGHT: Disney reads Davy Crockett's Journal.

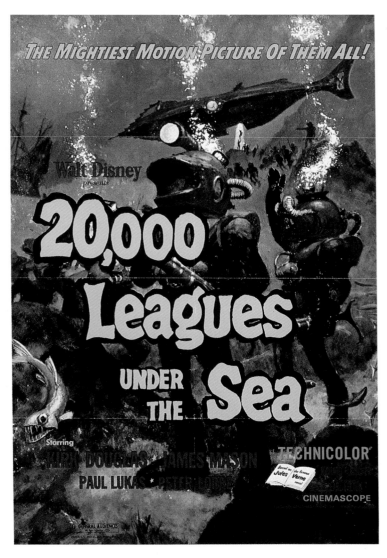

Davy Crockett, King of the Wild Frontier

1955

There is a memorable memo from the great movie producer David O Selznick upbraiding a studio executive for taking too much notice of what he is told by exhibitors. 'They were absolute death on what they called "Coonskin westerns,"' said Selznick. 'They were referring, of course, to westerns made with costumes that included the use of beaver hats . . . Then along came Walt Disney – who of course had more showmanship than 99 percent of exhibitors – and set the world on its ear with *Davy Crockett*.'

Yet Disney's triumph with *Davy Crockett* had less to do with the intrinsic merits of the movie than with Disney's courageous embracing of a new medium that at that time was regarded as the cinema's mortal enemy – television. Whereas the rest of the film industry was harrying itself to death to find gimmicks that would annihilate the competition of television (wider screens, greater length, more opulent color, more salacious material), Disney agreed to do a weekly show on television entitled *Disneyland*, which he would introduce himself. He needed the money to finance his own Disneyland project. Yet he would probably have agreed anyway. His reasoning was simple. Television gave him access to a huge audience – and he had always trusted the public on his films much more than the opinions of critics, executives or exhibitors – and while providing an audience for his past product television could help publicize his new films and ventures. There was some complaint that many of the programs amounted to little more than extended trailers for his new movies. Yet one such program, *Operation Undersea*, about the making of *20,000 Leagues Under the Sea*, was considered good enough to win a television Emmy award.

Particularly impressive is James Mason's complex, brooding Nemo, a haunted more than an evil character taking revenge on a world that has mistreated and undervalued his talents. Some have seen Mason's characterization as a portrait of the potentially dark side of Disney himself, a portrayal of what could have happened to his personality had his gifts not been recognized. A far-fetched proposition no doubt, but Disney might well have felt some sneaking sympathy for an innovator like Nemo who is scorned by less perceptive men and has to go to extreme lengths to demonstrate his powers.

For all the excellence of his performance, James Mason later commented drily that the real star of the film was the squid, a two-ton hydraulically operated monster, built by the same man who constructed the shark for *Jaws* and causing similar problems to those which Spielberg experienced with his sharp-toothed villain. The challenge for Disney was to outdo the famous squid fight in Cecil B DeMille's *Reap the Wild Wind* (1942). When the scene was first shot he and Fleischer were both disappointed with the results. 'Carry on with something else,' Disney told his director, 'we'll have to come back to this.' A more menacing monster was built, and the revised scene was now shot not against a placid pink sky as before, but against a violent storm. 'It made it a hundred times more expensive,' said Fleischer, 'but when we presented the idea to Walt, he said, "You're absolutely right, do it that way."' Disney knew that if the squid failed, so would the film. In the event it played its part to perfection, and *20,000 Leagues Under the Sea* was an enormous success.

In his first season on television, Disney's big hit was 'Davy Crockett,' a three-part drama which followed Crockett's progress from Indian fighter, to Congress, then finally to the Alamo. In casting the title role Disney had been recommended to watch the sci-fi horror film *Them!* (1954), with a view to offering the part of Crockett to one of the film's leading actors, James Arness, but Disney was more impressed by one of the co-stars, Fess Parker, who landed the role. (Arness went on to play Matt Dillon in the long-running television show 'Gunsmoke.')

During the shooting Disney asked his composer George Bruns and the writer Tom Blackburn to come up with a song that could be used as a recurring ballad, partly to pad out the length and partly to bridge the passage from one episode to another. Apologetically, and thirty minutes later, they came back and half-heartedly performed 'The Ballad of Davy Crockett' for Disney, who was understandably unimpressed but thought it would have to do. The record of the song was to soar to the top spot in the American charts and to stay there for the next three months.

The success of the song, coupled with the simple virtues of the television program, had a fantastic impact. Disney's fortunes were massively augmented by the merchandizing of material connected with the program. Posters, costumes, coloring books, wooden rifles were sold in phenomenal quantities. It was estimated that ten million Davy Crockett hats alone were sold during this time.

Given the fact that a sizeable proportion of the American public had seen *Davy Crockett* on television it might have seemed foolhardy of Disney to edit it into a film feature for the cinema. Also it risked looking old-fashioned alongside a new group of 1950s' westerns that were revising and refining the genre with considerable sophistication – films like the allegorical *High Noon* (1952), the mythic *Shane* (1953) and the psychologically tortured *The Naked Spur* (1952). Yet Disney again was proved right. Although it had been screened in black and white on television, it had been shot in color so it could be advantageously re-presented for the screen. In fact the film made a profit of $2½ million in America and spawned a sequel (which was also seen on TV first), *Davy Crockett and the River Pirates* (1956).

Of Disney's other western movies of the 1950s, *The Light in the Forest* (1958) was an attempt to adjust to the growing complexity of the genre by examining the theme of racial intolerance, but it emerged as tepid drama. Much better was *The Great Locomotive Chase* (1956), a producing opportunity for one of Disney's most reliable writers of the decade, Lawrence E Watkin, and telling a true story of the Civil War in which Northern soldiers had sneaked behind enemy lines to steal a train in order to sabotage the Southern rail supply line. No romantic interest – just straight pulsating action. The cast was headed by Jeffrey Hunter and, again, Fess Parker, but for the public Parker would always be Davy Crockett. As an actor he never did shed that coonskin hat.

ABOVE LEFT: Fess Parker played the title role in *Davy Crockett*.

ABOVE: Filming *The Great Locomotive Chase* (1956). The movie was based on the same incident which inspired the Buster Keaton classic, *The General*.

RIGHT: Fess Parker (left) and James MacArthur (right) in *The Light in the Forest* (1958), a historical film on the theme of racial integration.

Pollyanna
1960

Pollyanna was the first of five films Disney was to make starring Hayley Mills, whom he had snapped up sharply after her scene-stealing debut opposite her father John in the thriller *Tiger Bay* (1959). Disney probably felt he had discovered a new Shirley Temple for the subteen and grandparent audience at which his feature films at that time seemed primarily aimed. His choice of vehicle to exploit Miss Mills' talent was a remake of a 1920 Mary Pickford classic, based on the novel by Eleanor Porter.

Pollyanna (Hayley Mills) is a twelve-year-old orphan who goes to live with her rich aunt (Jane Wyman). She is an outspoken, fearless, fun-loving child who has a transforming impact on the people who come into contact with her, chipping off their crustiness and turning sour into sweet. It is a story about the triumph of innocence and, typically for Disney, the comic yet liberating effect of unstuffy vitality on restrained respectability. (*Lady and the Tramp* and *The Aristocats* have similar themes.)

For Disney, the material of *Pollyanna* was obviously congenial. Its rural cosiness and its period setting undoubtedly evoked the atmosphere of Disney's own childhood. Pollyanna is an orphan who gradually discovers a new family; the situation, or variations of it, is a common one in Disney. Pollyanna is also an individualist but one whose individualism has the effect not of challenging but of restoring and revitalizing traditional values. Her rebelliousness within a

ABOVE: Hayley Mills (right) made her American film debut in *Pollyanna* (1960), as the girl who befriends and charms everyone.

LEFT: Pollyanna arrives at her new home where her presence will soon make an impact on the local community.

RIGHT: Nancy Olson sells raffle tickets in *Pollyanna*.

LEFT: Hayley Mills as Pollyanna.

BELOW: A dual role for Hayley Mills in *The Parent Trap* (1961), playing twin daughters who are planning to re-unite their separated parents.

BOTTOM: Hayley Mills had her first screen romance, with Peter McEnery in *The Moon-Spinners* (1964), a thriller set in Crete.

RIGHT: A faith in invention: Fred MacMurray tries a new solution while his canine lab assistant observes intently, from *The Absent Minded Professor*.

family has the effect not of breaking it down but of waking it up. Just as the British had complained of the casting of an American boy in *Treasure Island*, so Americans would have been entitled to protest about the casting of an English girl for such a slice of Americana as *Pollyanna*, but most were quite enchanted by Hayley Mills in the title role. The enchantment carried over to the Motion Picture Academy who awarded her a special Oscar for her performance.

One might have expected the critical response to have matched the initial cynicism and grumpiness of the inhabitants of the film's small town, but Pollyanna's charm even seemed to cast its spell over the press. Admittedly one publication *(Monthly Film Bulletin)* brutally interpreted the movie as 'an incitement to child murder,' but such dubious sarcasm was generally untypical of the film's reception. As well as for Miss Mills there was praise for the strong supporting cast of Jane Wyman, Karl Malden, Nancy Olson, Donald Crisp, Adolphe Menjou and Agnes Moorehead. Apart from some doubts about the film's length of 133 minutes – sugary idealization should not perhaps be laid on so thickly – it was generally felt that writer-director David Swift had done a good job. Yet the film proved only a modest success rather than the smash hit predicted. Why?

Thinking about this later Disney felt that the story's sugary reputation had preceded the movie and possibly alienated some of its potential audience before they had seen it. He felt afterward that he should perhaps have changed the title so that the male audience, in particular, would not have felt so bashful about attending the film. Looking back at this period in an interview for the *New York Times*, Hayley Mills recalled how uncomfortable she was with this 'goody-goody' Pollyanna image, which she described as 'hideous.' Curiously the films she made for Disney after *Pollyanna* were less memorable but more profitable. The best of them are *The Parent Trap* (1961), in which she had a dual role playing twin sisters, and a thriller set in Greece, *The Moon-Spinners* (1964), in which less suspense is generated from Eli Wallach's villainy than from the film's interrogation of Hayley Mills' screen image. Is she a spunky tomboy or just a squealing teenager? Is she old enough, or for that matter attractive enough, to receive her first screen kiss? The film cleverly keeps you guessing.

The Absent Minded Professor
1961

The eponymous hero of *The Absent Minded Professor* is an amateur inventor who discovers an antigravitational substance called Flubber (flying rubber) which can give a bounce to the most jaded of basketball shoes and even turn an old Model T Ford into a UFO. Many have been moved to draw parallels between the film's hero and Disney himself – the simple small-town inventor with a vision, who is first laughed at by the bureaucrats and financiers but whose soaring success will change their attitude from skepticism to awe. If there was a concealed personal allegory amid the flubbery fun Disney would have been delighted by the film's fate – it pleased both public and press.

Some of the credit for the film must go to the unobtrusive ease of Robert Stevenson's direction (he had already shown himself to be a reliable Disney director through the success of *Old Yeller*). But the main plaudits were reserved for the leading performance of Fred MacMurray who was to become to Disney what James Stewart had been to Frank Capra

(a repository of the best American values) and second only to Mickey Mouse as Disney's favorite actor. He had already scored a hit for Disney with his role in *The Shaggy Dog* (1959), but his deft touch as the professor helped the film to become one of the most profitable light comedies in the studio's history. It prompted a sequel, *Son of Flubber* (1963), and a money-making rip-off, *The Love Bug* (1969), which is simply a variation of one of the earlier film's basic ideas (a car that likes to fly and has a mind of its own).

The strategy behind these comedies is simple. An element of fantasy is floated across domestic normality. These are films for families about families, but with a gimmick which, in the case of *The Absent Minded Professor*, was the old Disney standby of flight. 'We've always made things fly and defy gravity,' said Disney, who may have been thinking at the time of *Plane Crazy*, *Dumbo*, *Peter Pan* or even *Victory Through Air Power* (*Mary Poppins* was still to come). 'Now we've just gone on to floating football players and bouncing basketball players.' Actually Disney makes it sound much more routine than it appears on the screen. A scene where MacMurray helps his college team to victory by putting Flubber in their shoes gets more comedy out of basketball

than almost any movie prior to *One Flew Over the Cuckoo's Nest* (1975). One must also say that the special effects are quite spectacular – you will believe a man in a car can fly. Comedies are traditionally passed over when awards ceremonies come round, but *The Absent Minded Professor* had the not inconsiderable distinction of securing three Oscar nominations (for special effects, art direction and Edward Colman's black-and-white photography).

The fact that the film was making a heap of money while the costly *Sleeping Beauty* was losing a fortune was a lesson not lost on Disney. Maybe future financial success lay in the hands of low-budget comedy more than high-risk cartoon? The 1960s were to see quite a number of such comedies emanating from the Disney studios, but none with the charm of the sweetly surreal *The Absent Minded Professor*.

LEFT: Looking down on the White House: the Professor (Fred MacMurray) and his fiancée (Nancy Olson) soar over the nation's capital. From *The Absent Minded Professor*.

ABOVE RIGHT: The story of the absent minded but now fêted professor continues in *Son of Flubber*.

RIGHT: More aerial acrobatics in *Son of Flubber*, the highly successful sequel to *The Absent Minded Professor*.

Mary Poppins
1964

In film histories *Mary Poppins* tends to be wedged between the Oscar-winning *My Fair Lady* (1964) and the record-breaking *The Sound of Music* (1965), and many would argue that it has stood the test of time better than either of its rivals. Actually *Mary Poppins* was no slouch itself when it came to Oscars (it won five) or box-office performance (it was the biggest hit of Walt Disney's career). In many ways it is the summation of Disney's achievement, the film in which all he had learned about live-action filming, fantasy, animation and audiences all came together. It had four favorite ingredients that had often appeared in his best movies but never all together: a strong heroine, a splendid score, an English setting of the late nineteenth/early twentieth century, and the theme of flight. He must have thought he could not miss, and as history proves he did not.

Equally gratifying for Disney must have been the knowledge that the success of *Mary Poppins* was the fruition of twenty years' preparation. He had discovered the Mary Poppins stories through his daughter Diane in 1944 and, in that year, his brother Roy had met the authoress P L Travers, who was temporarily resident in New York after leaving England to escape the London blitz. She was very skeptical about the idea of a film and was not finally persuaded to sell the rights until 1960. The film had first been conceived of as a cartoon, but it was later decided to make it a combination of live-action and animation which Disney had not properly attempted since *So Dear to My Heart*.

Having obtained the rights, Disney now had to obtain a

ABOVE: Live action and animation merrily blended in *Mary Poppins*: Dick Van Dyke as Bert and Julie Andrews in the title role.

LEFT: The chimney-sweeps and Mary Poppins dance on the rooftops of London.

RIGHT: The Banks family: mother (Glynis Johns), father (David Tomlinson) and their two children (Karen Dotrice and Matthew Garber).

Mary Poppins. Extraordinarily, in retrospect, one of the actresses considered was Bette Davis. By a curious coincidence a year after *Mary Poppins* Miss Davis was to play an English nanny in the superb British horror movie *The Nanny* (1965), and the mental exercise of imagining Miss Davis's characterization in the world of Mary Poppins is both fascinating and disorienting. Another candidate was Mary Martin who at least had the advantage of being able to sing. Julie Andrews came into the picture when Disney saw her on the stage in *Camelot* and, so the story goes, he was quite entranced by the way she whistled. She was much younger than the Mary Poppins of the stories, but Disney thought that might be an advantage rather than a disadvantage. The other problem was that Miss Andrews was eager to repeat her stage triumph of Eliza Doolittle in *My Fair Lady* on screen and wanted to wait until Warner Brothers had completed casting for their film to see if she had landed the role. Disney had waited almost twenty years for P L Travers to make up her mind; he could wait a few months for Jack Warner. When the role of Eliza eventually, and controversially, went to Audrey Hepburn, Julie Andrews was free to do *Mary Poppins*. In one of the ironies so beloved by Hollywood, Julie Andrews was to win an Oscar for her performance while Audrey Hepburn was not even to be nominated for hers.

Now that he had the Mary Poppins he wanted, Disney was confident that he could assemble the ideal personnel to do justice to the material. The choice of director was simple. Robert Stevenson was not only one of Disney's most reliable filmmakers; he was also English by birth and had been brought up by a nanny in Edwardian England, so he could be trusted to have a special feeling for the material. One might also remember that Stevenson had once directed a very good film version of *Jane Eyre* (1944) in the year before Disney first came across the Mary Poppins stories, so he might have a special empathy for the feelings of a strong heroine in the position of a servant in a household of rather stiff, conventional values. Also it rapidly became clear to Disney that Richard and Robert Sherman were excelling themselves in providing attractive songs. There was the ultimate Disney tongue twister, 'Supercalifragilisticexpialidocious'; a charmer for the heroine, 'A Spoonful of Sugar'; a haunting one for the chimney-sweep, Bert, 'Chim Chim Cher-ee' (which was to win an Oscar); and a big production number 'Jolly Holiday,' which was to provide the movie's liveliest combination of choreography and cartoon. Disney's own

favorite song in the score was 'Feed the Birds,' which would frequently reduce him to tears and which he confidently predicted would displace Brahms's Lullaby in popularity.

The other important roles – David Tomlinson as the stiff banker Mr Banks who is to be humanized by Mary, and Glynis Johns as his suffragette wife – seem perfectly cast. More arguable is Dick Van Dyke's Bert, not because of his song-and-dance capabilities, of course, but because of his excruciating cockney accent. It is a blot on the movie but not a serious one – many Disney cartoons have survived the unfortunate accents of their stars.

One of the things which possibly helped the popularity of *Mary Poppins* was its fortuitous timing. When it appeared, far from seeming old-fashioned, it had many elements in common with contemporary cinematic trends, but the novelty was that it gave them a positive rather than negative connotation. A brilliant rooftop dance number evokes a similar scene in *West Side Story* (1961), for example, but in the

Disney scene it is a choreographic rendering of joy, not conflict. Thematically *Mary Poppins* has much in common with Alfred Hitchcock's *The Birds* (1963) – something comes out of the sky to shock a staid community's complacency – but the effect is benevolent rather than terrifying. (Intriguingly Disney's old collaborator, Ub Iwerks, worked on the Hitchcock film, which makes use of a Disneyesque combination of live-action, animation and special effects.) In contrast to two sinister movies about master/servant relationships, Losey's *The Servant* (1963) and Wyler's *The Collector* (1965), Disney's eponymous heroine not only carries her servitude lightly but completely transforms both parents and children with a broom of pure wholesomeness.

The novelty of all this was undoubtedly enhanced by Julie Andrews' performance. She brings wit and warmth to the character and a sprightly rather than starchy independence. At the time she seemed quite a new kind of screen heroine – clean, tomboyish, unsexy and yet, as the critic Molly Haskell astutely noted, 'a little ruthless in her ladylike pursuit of her ambitions.' She comes down from on high to fulfill the children's fantasies but she also brusquely forges a new marriage out of the husband's capitalism and the wife's femininity. In retrospect the character now looks a rum combination of a feminine Shane and a fantasy Margaret Thatcher.

The main theme of *Mary Poppins* is not dissimilar to that of *Peter Pan*. A magical personage descends on an unhappy household, bringing joy to the children and harmony and wonder back into the lives of a mercenary father and a militant mother. It waved a similar magic wand over the most hardened critics, who gave Disney his best notices for decades. When this was expanded into public and industry acclaim, with huge attendances and no fewer than thirteen Oscar nominations (only one movie, *All About Eve*, 1950, has ever secured more), Disney's cup was full. The final part of his career had at last achieved its ultimate vindication.

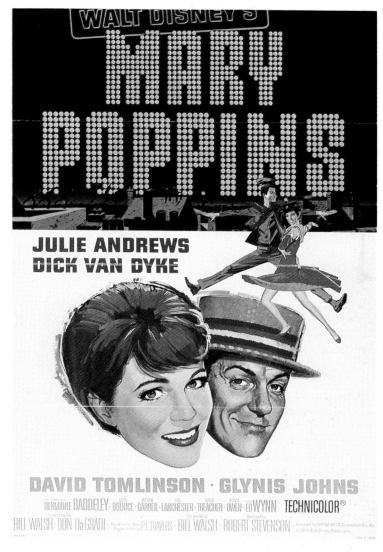

ABOVE FAR LEFT: Riding the carousel horses in *Mary Poppins*.

ABOVE LEFT: 'It's a Jolly Holiday': Julie Andrews, Dick Van Dyke and four dancing penguin waiters.

LEFT: The laughing sequence: gales of hilarity lift Ed Wynn to the ceiling.

ABOVE RIGHT: The poster for *Mary Poppins*.

RIGHT: Stars and producer arrive for the glittering premiere of *Mary Poppins* at Grauman's Chinese Theater: Julie Andrews (left), Walt Disney (center), Dick Van Dyke (right) and cartoon support.

ADIEU
A WALT
DISNEY

N° 924 / 24 DÉCEMBRE 1966 / 1,20 F

Le soir même
de la disparition de
Walt Disney un de ses
proches collaborateurs a
réalisé pour « Paris-Match »
ce dessin qui est
l'adieu de Mickey à
son papa.

CHAPTER FOUR

Would Walt Have Approved?

Disney Films after the Death of Walt – 1967 to the Present

Walt Disney died from lung cancer on 15 December 1966. More than twenty years after his death his spirit still pervades the Disney studios. 'His picture is everywhere,' wrote one commentator after a visit to the Studio in 1982, 'in the entrances to buildings, in the hallways, in the executive offices.' His personal achievement is still celebrated through the phenomenon of Disneyland, the television programs with their seemingly inexhaustible supply of brilliant movie clips, and the shrewd re-release every seven years or so of the major cartoon features. *Cinderella* has been around five times since its original release in 1950, always successfully. In 1987 *Snow White and the Seven Dwarfs* was re-released in America on its fiftieth anniversary – it was an immediate box-office hit.

Yet the Disney organization has also awakened to the need for change, particularly in the 1980s. 'The problem,' according to production chief Thomas Wilhite in 1982, 'is to walk the line between maintaining what was good in the past and to acknowledge that there has been a tremendous change in the movie audience in the last ten to fifteen years.' People who grew up in the turbulent 1960s, Wilhite argued, are parents now themselves and 'raising their children with a different point of view.'

In what ways have the old traditions of the past been maintained? Whatever one might think of more recent product in comparison with the mighty quintet of masterpieces between 1937 and 1942, the Disney Studio still leads the field in the sphere of the feature-length cartoon. There have been rivals in the field, such as *The Lord of the Rings* (1978) or *Watership Down* (1978) or Jim Henson–Frank Oz extravaganzas like *The Dark Crystal* (1983) but none has challenged the Disney supremacy. Indeed the main challenge has come from within. In 1979 in a development that recalled the bitter strike at the studio in 1941, seventeen of the studio's top animators, led by Don Bluth, handed in their notice and went on to form their own company. According to Bluth the Disney motto of 'Be creative, so long as you do what you're told . . .' was just too oppressive. Bluth has gone on to make two impressive features, *The Secret of NIMH* (1982) and *An American Tail* (1986) which frankly do not look that different from the usual Disney product, barring a new harshness of tone. On the other hand the film that was interrupted and delayed by the walkout, *The Fox and the Hound* (1981), went on to win critical plaudits and become Disney's biggest-grossing, first-run animation film ever.

Up to the late 1970s the policy on live-action features seemed much as Walt Disney had left it. Nearly all the movies were modest family comedies, with a touch of fantasy

LEFT: A vivid impression by *Paris Match* of the impact of Disney's death: Mickey Mouse weeps for his creator.

RIGHT: The 'Nine Old Men,' who carried on the Disney tradition: from left to right, Milt Kahl, Wolfgang Reitherman, Marc Davis, Les Clark, Frank Thomas, Ward Kimball, Eric Larson, John Lounsbery, Ollie Johnston.

or adventure. It seemed to be paying off – after all, *The Love Bug* was the biggest-grossing movie of 1969. So on trundled the familiar fluff – *Bedknobs and Broomsticks* (1971), *The Island at the Top of the World* (1974), *One of Our Dinosaurs Is Missing* (1975), *Pete's Dragon* (1977), *Candleshoe* (1977), and other films as equally, painlessly forgettable as these, in some of which Jodie Foster was being improbably groomed as the Hayley Mills of the 1970s. Just occasionally, as had happened with *The Absent Minded Professor* in the 1960s, along came a comedy with an intriguing idea – like *Freaky Friday* (1976), about the domestic, social and sexual complications that ensue when there is an unaccountable change of personalities between mother (Barbara Harris) and daughter (Jodie Foster). Mainly, though, the movies were barely distinguishable in one's mind – as light and as clean as a soap-bubble, and about as substantial.

However, if tradition were being maintained, it was at the kind of price Walt would not have tolerated – namely, that the Disney Studio was missing out. While the moviemakers at Disney continued to be anonymous technicians with little

personality, the other studios were responding to the era of the movie superbrats and were being rewarded with smash hits like Coppola's *The Godfather* (1972), Lucas's *American Graffiti* (1973), Spielberg's *Jaws* (1975) and De Palma's *Carrie* (1976). Operations at Disney were ticking along smoothly enough, but *Jaws* had startled the industry by making it aware of the potential size of the audience out there. It was not enough anymore for a movie to be a success – it had to be a blockbusting mega-hit.

The goldmine of George Lucas's *Star Wars* (1977) for Fox must have had a stunning impact on the Disney organization, not least because they were one of the studios that had turned it down. *Star Wars* gathered into its embrace a completely new child and teenage audience (an audience that Disney had previously thought was theirs); out-Disneyed Disney in the audacity of its merchandising; and in the movie provided a technological display that made previously admired Disneyesque special effects look suddenly quaint and feeble. From a studio that used to initiate trends and anticipate or create audience tastes, the Disney product now looked a little

ABOVE LEFT: One of Disney's biggest hits of the 1960s, *The Love Bug*, about a Volkswagen with a mind of its own.

ABOVE: A dinosaur's skeleton becomes the focal point of a search for a secret strip of microfilm, in *One of Our Dinosaurs Is Missing*.

LEFT: Angela Lansbury and David Tomlinson starred in *Bedknobs and Broomsticks*, a story set in England during World War II and mixing live action and animation.

ABOVE RIGHT: A scene from *Condorman* (1980), a fantasy that never quite got off the ground.

RIGHT: The orphan, Pete, and his dragon, Elliott, who can disappear at will: Sean Marshall (left) and dragon in *Pete's Dragon*.

LEFT: The affection of Disney
Productions for stories of
Victorian England was again
evident in *The Great Mouse
Detective*, a rodent version of
Arthur Conan Doyle.

BELOW: After the quaint, modest
family comedies of the previous
two decades, Disney Studios in
the 1980s moved into the age of
cinematic computerized hi-tech
with *Tron*.

RIGHT: A monstrously expensive
production, *The Black Cauldron*
did not fare as well as hoped.

old-fashioned and was sometimes caught chasing a band-wagon that had already passed by. Should not Disney's *The Black Hole* (1979) have come before *Star Wars*, not tamely after it? Commendable of them to snap up director Carroll Ballard for *Never Cry Wolf* after his success with *The Black Stallion* (1979), but should they not have snapped up *The Black Stallion* to begin with? The figures told their own story. Between 1976 and 1981, Disney's share of the American box-office fell from seven percent to four percent. Movies were making less for them than merchandising and theme-parks.

Over the last decade there has been an always fascinating, though not always successful, attempt to accommodate and adjust the Disney product to the new generation of film audiences. The name 'Disney' still connotes a certain kind of entertainment, one that promises fun and fantasy for all the family. *The Great Mouse Detective* (1986), a cartoon Conan Doyle, and *The Flight of the Navigator* (1986), a boy's adventure with a spaceship that became the first American movie to be nostalgic for the Jimmy Carter era, are honorable continuations of that tradition. Even the failures in the fantasy field, like the bloated *The Black Cauldron* (1985) and the clever but charmless *Return to Oz* (1985) have had their moments of spectacle and imagination.

More significantly there has been a bold shift in subject and style. In the early 1980s Disney dabbled in horror (*The Watcher in the Woods*, 1981; *Something Wicked This Way Comes*, 1983), and in a co-production with Paramount sword and sorcery (*Dragonslayer*, 1981), and even outright eccentricity (*Popeye*, 1980). If there was wide disagreement over the merits of the film there was none over their disappointing – in some cases, disastrous – commercial performance. Yet they at least revived two valuable attributes of the golden days of Disney – the ability to startle as well as soothe, and a willingness to throw caution to the winds. *Tron* (1982) was a modern-tech movie that not only dragged Disney kicking and screaming into the twentieth century but right bang into the computer age. It never really found a plot or character on which to hang its spectacular optical effects and computer graphics and its thunder was to be stolen by *War Games* (1983), but it was still an impressive technical display. Disney had found the hardware at last; it had only to remember where it had put its heart.

The studio also relocated and redefined its appeal to the

teenage audience. Tim Hunter's film of S E Hinton's *Tex* (1982), starring Matt Dillon, had two remarkable characteristics for a Disney film – four-letter words, and the fact that it was a *succès d'estime*. With Ron Howard's *Splash!* (1984), however, they at last hit the box-office jackpot. More recently the diversification into Touchstone Films, for the release of Disney films aimed primarily at adult audiences, has attracted talents of the caliber of Martin Scorsese, Bette Midler, Richard Dreyfuss and Paul Mazursky, and resulted in hit movies like *Down and Out in Beverly Hills* (1986), *The Color of Money* (1986), *Outrageous Fortune* (1987) and *Tin Men* (1987).

Most film histories about Disney stop at the maestro's death, yet there is a whole new generation of moviegoers who must feel closer to and more familiar with the recent Disney products than the classics of the past, so it would be churlish to exclude them. This chapter also includes such movies as *Never Cry Wolf* and *Something Wicked This Way Comes* which are regarded by some commentators as the worst, not the best, of Disney. However, box-office receipts do not always tell the truth, and these movies have considerable merits in their own right. They also serve as provocative examples of the way the Disney organization has attempted to reconcile the virtues of the past with the vicissitudes of the present in the twenty years after Disney's death.

Would Walt have approved? For the most part, I think so.

The Aristocats
1970

On the basis of some sketches by Ken Anderson, Disney had given the go-ahead to *The Aristocats* before he died; and as the animation was mainly in the hands of the Disney veterans directed by Wolfgang Reitherman, it is clear that the film intended to follow the traditions so clearly established by the master. The film is set in Paris in 1910 and the plot concerns an aristocratic cat and her three kittens whose lives are in danger from a villainous butler who wishes to supplant the privileged position of the cats in his mistress's will. The storyline has many echoes of other Disney movies – a bit of *Lady and the Tramp* when the rascally O'Malley cat appears on the scene plus a bit of *101 Dalmatians* in the threats to animals from greedy, grasping humans.

Most of the humor comes not from the main characters but from minor figures who crop up in cameo roles, like the two dogs Napoleon and Lafayette (Pat Buttram and George Lindsey) who make Edgar the butler's life a misery; or a typically loyal mouse (mice are invariably presented affectionately in Disney, for obvious reasons); and two English geese walking to Paris, who enliven the film without furthering the action and who are voiced by Monica Evans and Carole Shelley. Musically the highlight is a set-piece led by one of O'Malley's friends, Scat-Cat (Scatman Crothers), called 'Every Body Wants To Be A Cat,' which is distinguished by flashy animation, dizzy color contrasts and a style that seems emulous of the rhythmic bounce of *Sweet Charity* (1969). 'It isn't Beethoven, mama, but it sure bounces,' says one of the kittens, which might be a cheeky reference to Walt Disney's own famous remark about the animation of the Pastoral Symphony in *Fantasia*: 'Gee, this'll really *make* Beethoven.'

American jazz in what is supposed to be the Paris of 1910? This kind of anachronism is not uncommon in Disney but is rather glaring in *The Aristocats* because of the stylistic inconsistency of other parts of the film. The French setting is suggested by a Maurice Chevalier title song and by the names. However, by the time we have encountered American voices for the kittens, accents of the Deep South for the two dogs, English geese and Phil Harris as O'Malley, the Parisian context has been completely nullified, which is a shame because some of it is beautifully drawn. Similarly, when he learns of his possible inheritance, dollar signs flash into Edgar's eyes – in which case, what is the point of characterizing him as an *English* butler in *Paris*? Part of the time the film seems unsure about whether to have its eye on its characters or its audience, and the inconsistencies are a little irritating.

Overall *The Aristocats* is rather an uneven achievement – ironically so, since, by all accounts Reitherman altered the Disney practice of making individual animators responsible for different individual sequences, and tried to bring everything together into a cohesive whole before the final animation began. Some of the backgrounds lack detail and depth – the opening scenes with O'Malley, in particular, seem to play against the limpest of studio backdrops. At other stages however, like the chase with the dogs and the fight in the barn, the animation has the familiar panache. The overall effect is distinctively Disney, which was clearly a major aim, and it is certainly likeable, even while it stutters rather than startles and seems a bit lacking in confidence. It is understandable that Disney's survivors are still feeling his legacy as a great but somewhat intimidating one.

LEFT: 'Everybody wants to be a cat': Scat Cat's group enjoying a jam session on the Left Bank.

ABOVE RIGHT: Edgar the butler with Madame and her precious cats.

RIGHT: Duchess with her kittens, Toulouse and Berlioz.

ABOVE LEFT: Edgar the butler hatches an evil plan when he learns that he will inherit a fortune if anything happens to Madame's cats. From *The Aristocats*.

LEFT: 'You're too much, Duchess,' says O'Malley when she plays the harp for him in *The Aristocats*.

ABOVE: Edgar's plan to drown the cats is beginning to backfire.

RIGHT: Some of the movie's best comedy is provided by the country dogs, Napoleon and Lafayette, who provide a foil for Edgar's villainy.

FAR LEFT: A cat's best friend: the loyal mouse, Roquefort. From *The Aristocats*.

LEFT: Edgar the butler with members of Scat Cat's band during the memorable mayhem in the barn.

BELOW LEFT: O'Malley comforts Duchess and her kittens.

RIGHT: The lady and the tramp revisited: romance blossoms between O'Malley and Duchess.

BELOW: Feline feelings of love in a romantic, moonlit Paris.

Robin Hood
1973

What would Walt Disney have made of this version of *Robin Hood*? There was no reason why it should not continue the Disney tradition, since many of the chief personnel involved in the movie were veterans from Disney's heyday. It was Ken Anderson, one of the most experienced art directors and character designers on the Disney lot (famous, in particular, for once having inadvertently set fire to Disney's mustache) who had first proposed the idea of an animated version of *Robin Hood*. The story and script had then been developed by Larry Clemmons, one of the writers on *The Jungle Book*; and the direction was in the vastly experienced hands of Wolfgang Reitherman. Yet there were certain features of the movie that filled Disney purists with alarm and still look questionable today.

It is interesting to speculate whether Walt Disney would even have liked the basic idea. He had already done this legend, live-action style, in *The Story of Robin Hood and His Merrie Men*; and, as we have seen from *Three Little Pigs* and his resistance to the idea of a follow-up to *Mary Poppins*, he was not enamored of the idea of sequels. This new version inevitably has some of the same events of the earlier one, including the obligatory archery contest; and one wonders whether the chief animators at Disney at this time were toying with the idea of doing a series of animated versions of Disney's live-action films. If so, nothing was to come of it, which makes this new *Robin Hood* seem more anomalous than ever. Yet it must be said that the film was very popular, and there was no slacking in the high standard of animation nor the careful attention to story-editing. Although some impressive preliminary sketches were done for the character of King Richard the Lion-Hearted, it was felt finally that there was no room for him in the overall structure of the film

ABOVE: Filming *Robin Hood* using a multiplane camera.

LEFT: Ollie Johnston working on the drawings and character of Prince John.

TOP RIGHT: Robin Hood and Prince John.

RIGHT: A story meeting.

and he was relegated to a short section at the end of the film. When it came to eliminating even excellent draughtsmanship if it impeded the flow of the story, the new regime were clearly determined to be just as decisive and strict as Walt himself had been.

The main novelty of this version of *Robin Hood* is that all the characters are represented as animals. Robin is a fox, Little John a bear, Prince John a lion, Alan-a-Dale a rooster, and so on. This works quite well in visual terms and contributes considerably to the humor. For example Prince John is a nailbiting, neurotic lion rather than a noble one, who occasionally roars but is more often given to whimpering for his 'mummy.' By contrast, his adviser Sir Hiss ('Hypnosis will rid you of your psychosis, sire') has all the slinkiness and guile that one traditionally associates with the snake. It is Sir Hiss who has hypnotized King Richard and sent him away on that 'crazy Crusade.' The snake has not only the best animation, as in *The Jungle Book*, but also all the best lines ('A mere slip of the forked tongue,' he says to reassure the Prince at one stage), and the part is convincingly and enthusiastically played by Terry-Thomas.

The script of *Robin Hood* is a witty one and very well interpreted by the cast but, as with *The Jungle Book*, questions were raised about the relation between animation and voice characterization, and which should come first. For some critics the voice personalities of Peter Ustinov (as Prince John) and Phil Harris (as Little John) were so strong as

ABOVE: Little John and Robin Hood in Sherwood Forest.

LEFT: Minstrel rooster Alan-a-Dale finds a lethal use for his lute, with the help of Friar Tuck.

ABOVE RIGHT: The theft of Prince John's gold.

RIGHT: Serenade in Sherwood Forest.

virtually to overwhelm the animation. In fact Ollie Johnston freely conceded that his animated interpretation of Prince John was heavily influenced by Ustinov's pre-recorded vocal performance. Similarly one cannot forget that Sir Hiss is played by Terry-Thomas because the snake is even given the actor's most distinctive characteristic – a gap between its teeth. If one is constantly seeing Ustinov in Prince John and Terry-Thomas in Sir Hiss, one is equally seeing Baloo the Bear in Little John because of the overpowering distinctiveness of Phil Harris's voice. Even Monica Evans (as Maid Marian) and Carole Shelley (as Lady Kluck) do a vocal variation on their double-act as the English geese in *The Aristocats*. With such a bewildering cluster of associations getting in the way of the characterization of *Robin Hood*, one sometimes cannot see Sherwood Forest for the trees.

It must be emphasized that it is not simply the distinctive voices that distract – it is the clash of voices. This was a problem in *The Aristocats* and is even more acute here, since one is dealing with famous mythological/actual characters. For example we have an English Robin Hood (a role well taken by Brian Bedford), but an American Little John and even an American Friar Tuck. Andy Devine is an entertaining Tuck but one feels like asking what the driver of John Ford's *Stagecoach* (1939) is doing in Sherwood Forest. Prince John and Sir Hiss are English, but Alan-a-Dale is a balladeer who, as vocalized by Roger Miller, would be more welcome in Nashville than Nottingham.

The Disney animators would no doubt argue that this sort of inner consistency is not demanded by the kind of audiences at whom the film is aimed. This is fair enough and if one is not disconcerted by some of the voice characterizations and the clash of styles, then *Robin Hood* is certainly entertaining. The older Disney fan might feel the absence of a memorable song and be disorientated by the lack of stylistic integration, but the younger admirer will probably be swept up in the adventure. They still know how to tell a story.

The Rescuers

1977

A young girl, Penny, has been captured by the notorious Madame Medusa who needs the assistance of a child small enough to crawl through the entrance and retrieve for her the precious Devil's Eye Diamond. However, Penny has smuggled out a message of help, and it comes to the notice of the Rescue Aid Society, which meets, pointedly enough, in the basement of the United Nations building in New York. Two of the rescuers, Bernard (Bob Newhart) and Bianca (Eva Gabor), are assigned to help Penny who is being held in Devil's Bayou in the Louisiana swamplands. They are uncomfortably transported by Orville who is the pilot and indeed sole member of the Albatross Air Service and whose flight accommodation is somewhat primitive, consisting of a sardine tin tied to his back. (Is this a Disney dig at American airlines?) They are also assisted by a delightful dragonfly called Evinrude and opposed by Madame Medusa's deadly alligator henchmen, Nero and Brutus.

Opinion has tended to be divided on *The Rescuers*. 'The people who really need rescuing are the Disney animators,' said one critic. Those who disliked it tended to feel it was derivative and a concoction of unimaginatively brewed segments from well-tried Disney formulae such as friendly mice and a *femme fatale* as a villainess. Some also felt that the contemporary setting of the film did not work to its advantage, as it seemed incongruous and essentially irrelevant to the plot. It was as if the Disney organization was simply animating the formula of its live-action – and by this time, rather jaded – comedy thrillers.

However, *The Rescuers* also had its champions who found it the most exciting Disney cartoon since *101 Dalmatians*. It had two advantages over developments since *The Jungle Book* – the personality of the characters resided in the drawings,

not the voices; and the subject was treated as pure fantasy and not as the imitation of human action in animal skins. Madame Medusa was also felt to be a fine villainess, and Geraldine Page's characterization was actually a performance and not simply a display of personality.

There is something to be said for both points of view, and the reason for it is that *The Rescuers* was undoubtedly a transitional work between *Robin Hood* and *The Fox and the Hound*. In 1973 the Disney organization had employed a new group of animators to train them in the traditions of Disney excellence, to foster fresh ideas, and particularly to groom them to replace the existing chief animators, many of whom had been with Disney since the 1930s and were approaching retirement. 'The new team have the same kind of energy and drive we had in the 1930s,' said Ken Anderson, 'nothing is beyond them.' In fact there was to be a certain amount of friction caused by this infusion of new blood, culminating in the walkout of 1979 led by Don Bluth who complained of the lack of leadership and of the kind of carelessness which, he said, had resulted in his being told not to waste time drawing in the whites of one of the character's eyes in *The Rescuers*.

The Rescuers is essentially the swan song of the group of top veteran animators whom Walt used to refer to as the 'Nine Old Men.' Four of them – Les Clark, Marc Davis, Ward Kimball and Eric Larson – had either retired from animation by the mid-1970s or moved to another department in the Disney organization. Three of the chief animators on *The Rescuers* – Ollie Johnston, Milt Kahl and Frank Thomas – let it be known that this would be their last feature-length cartoon. One of the co-directors, John Lounsbery, who had worked for Disney for forty years, died before the film was completed. Only one of the nine, Wolfgang Reitherman, was to have his name on the next cartoon feature, *The Fox and the Hound. The Rescuers* seems poised between two worlds: fresh in its animation but thematically a reprise of old themes; a simultaneous requiem and resurrection.

BELOW LEFT: Penny is ordered by the evil Madame Medusa to help her in her search for a precious diamond.

RIGHT: The friendly and daring dragonfly, Evinrude.

BELOW: Fly with my airline at your own peril: Bernard and Bianca with their pilot Orville, who *is* the Albatross Air Service.

The Fox and the Hound
1981

Although under the overall supervision of Wolfgang Reitherman, *The Fox and the Hound* was largely the work of animators who had joined the studio after Walt Disney's death (the credited directors are Art Stevens, Ted Berman and Richard Rich). It might be this that gives the film such vivacity. The newcomers clearly wanted to demonstrate that while they respected and honored the traditions of Disney animation, they had some inventive ideas of their own. Critically and commercially, it remains the best received of all the studio's feature-length cartoons made since Walt died.

Based on a novel by Daniel P Mannix, *The Fox and the Hound* tells the story of a fox cub, Tod (Mickey Rooney), who is adopted by the kindly Widow Tweed (Jeanette Nolan). At the same time her neighbor, Amos (Jack Albertson), has purchased a hound puppy, Copper (Kurt Russell). The two animals grow up the best of friends. However, this changes when Copper is taken away by Amos to be trained as a hunting hound. He returns with an older dog, Chief (Pat Buttram), and they chase after Tod, a chase that almost ends in tragedy when Chief is knocked off a trestle by a train and his leg is broken. Copper vows revenge on Tod.

Freed by Widow Tweed to respond to the call of the wild and learn to fend for himself, Tod is looked after by a wise owl called Big Mama (Pearl Bailey) and a vixen, Vixey (Sandy Duncan). However, Amos enters the woods and starts to lay traps. When he is attacked by a bear and when Copper is also injured when trying to help, Tod leaps to the rescue. In a pulsating finale Copper must decide between obedience to his master in seeking Tod's death or a reaffirmation of friendship by saving Tod's life.

The movie's basic plot has a great deal in common with the British movie *The Belstone Fox* (1973), but in Disney terms the ambience is very close to a classic like *Bambi*. Here again we have a harsh portrayal of man as hunter, a depiction of animal rivalry, the themes of parental loss, adoption, and growth, and a similar attention to the changing seasons. The critic Richard Corliss thought it a 'return to primal Disney, to the glory days of the early features when the forces of evil and nature conspired to wrench strong new emotions out of toddlers and brooding concern from their parents . . . it confronts the Dostoevskian terrors of the heart.'

It must have been at least forty years since a Disney film had been compared with Dostoevsky, yet in a curious way it is not inappropriate. Dostoevsky was obsessed with the duality of man, and the love/hate conflict in this movie between the fox and the hound, coupled with the way each seems to oscillate between roles of hunter and quarry, predator and victim, certainly contains aspects of this 'double' theme. Can Copper the hound reconcile his own instinctive nature with his gradually acquired love for Tod the fox? One thinks of

BELOW LEFT: The Widow Tweed adopts a fox cub.

RIGHT: Early games between the fox Tod, and the hound Copper, who have become firm friends.

BELOW: The odd couple: Copper and Tod. Soon the ingrained prejudice of maturity will replace the instinctive innocence of childhood.

ABOVE: Big Mama, the owl, has a word with Boomer, the woodpecker, and Dinky, the sparrow. From *The Fox and the Hound*.

LEFT: Tod and Vixey. Vixey will educate him in the ways of the forest.

ABOVE RIGHT: Man has entered the forest: Amos, the hunter, tries to shoot Tod.

RIGHT: Former friends now confront each other as enemies.

Orson Welles's parable about the scorpion and the frog in *Mr Arkadin* (1955), which argues that there is no logic in character but also no escaping one's own nature. One thinks also of that great moment in Mark Twain's *The Adventures of Huckleberry Finn* when Huck struggles with his conscience in deciding whether or not to reveal the whereabouts of Jim, who is a runaway slave but also the boy's friend.

If references to Dostoevsky, Orson Welles and Mark Twain seem rather heavy in the context of a discussion of an animated cartoon, the only defense is that *The Fox and the Hound* is an unusually substantial animated cartoon. It seems to be reaching out for a new Disney audience – a more mature, reflective one perhaps – and attempting to banish the usual Disney undeserved image of mindless middle-brow mawkishness. At the same time it endeavors to retain the allegiance of those who have remained faithful to the Disney product because it is wholesome family entertainment and because of its sense of fun. One of the ways of doing this (something undoubtedly learned from the Disney veterans) is to pepper the supporting characters with a lot of comedy characteristics and business – a badger (John McIntire) who is infuriated when his routine is disturbed, or the endearingly lugubrious Chief cunningly determined to wring the maximum amount of sympathy and relaxation from the situation of having his leg in splints. There is a particularly mischievous running joke in which Boomer the woodpecker and Dinky the sparrow try unsuccessfully to trap a most affable

caterpillar called Squeaks. Squeaks becomes a glowworm briefly when he has a shocking collision with an electric pylon but finally blossoms into a beautiful butterfly.

The major suspense set-pieces are the scene in which Chief's leg is broken, the excitement conveyed by drawing the train in a way that makes its appearance seem more and more menacing, and the final fight with the bear which is all probing close-ups and furious movement. A token, unhelpful song is the only real blemish. Mainly, *The Fox and the Hound* is a gripping narrative, equally well characterized by actors and animators, truly a film for children of all ages.

Never Cry Wolf
1983

Never Cry Wolf might seem to represent a return by the Disney organization to the world of the True-Life Adventure series. Indeed one of the film's producers, Jack Couffer, began his movie career with a photography assignment on *The Living Desert*. However, the approach to the material is very different from those earlier films – tougher in tone and more authentic in style.

Based on the factual reminiscences of the Canadian author Farley Mowat, *Never Cry Wolf* tells the story of a young biologist, Tyler (Charles Martin Smith), who has been sent by the Canadian government to study the behavior of Arctic wolves. The government is seeking confirmation that the wolves are responsible for the destruction of the region's herds of caribou in order to justify its policy of extermination. However, Tyler's research begins to cast doubt on whether the wolves are destroying the caribou for food (he begins to believe the wise old Eskimo who is convinced that, in only attacking sick caribous, the wolves might actually be helping to preserve the species). He also finds himself becoming more and more sympathetic to the animals.

There is a certain amount of Disneyesque cuteness in *Never Cry Wolf*. The scene where Tyler falls through a frozen lake is treated more as knockabout comedy than as a potentially fatal disaster. Tyler adopts two wolves with their three pups and names them 'George' and 'Angelina.' He has come to the conclusion that the wolves feed more on mice than on caribou, and, to test his theory that this is a sufficiently sustaining diet, Tyler munches through his own 'mouseburger' while the distinctly quizzical wolves watch.

Yet there is also a harsher edge to the film. Tyler encounters a bush pilot (Brian Dennehy) and an Eskimo (Samson Jorah) who are out to make money from the selling of

ABOVE LEFT: Tod bravely confronts a ferocious bear.

LEFT: The huge black bear advances on Amos.

ABOVE RIGHT: Zachary Ittimangnaq makes his screen debut as an Eskimo who befriends the biologist in *Never Cry Wolf*.

RIGHT: Lining up a shot of the hero (Charles Martin Smith, crouching by the rock) in *Never Cry Wolf*.

LEFT: The Arctic wolves in *Never Cry Wolf*.

BELOW: The biologist Tyler (Charles Martin Smith, left) persuades a bush pilot (Brian Dennehy) to fly him out to the wilderness where he can begin his study.

RIGHT: Arriving in the wilderness.

BELOW RIGHT: Tyler begins to observe the behavior of the wolves.

wolf skins – one is reminded of both *Bambi* (man's violation of nature) and *101 Dalmatians* (the killing of dogs for Cruella's overcoats). 'Beautiful country – limitless opportunities,' says the pilot, and it is clear that he equates beauty with economic exploitation. When 'George' and 'Angelina' disappear and the Eskimo reappears some time later with a new row of immaculate white teeth, we are left to draw our own conclusion – that the animals have been killed to finance the Eskimo's dental work, and these shiny teeth are a symbol of human rapaciousness. The movie's ecological theme is to move toward the end to one of misanthropy, as Tyler, sickened by human greed and rather like the John Wayne character at the end of Ford's *The Searchers* (1956), renounces civilization in favor of the wilderness.

The introduction of the Eskimo characters inevitably prompts a comparison with Robert Flaherty's classic 1922 movie, *Nanook of the North*. Indeed the Eskimo Ootek, played by Zachary Ittimangnaq, is even referred to as 'Nanook' at one stage. It is a brave filmmaker who would court comparison with Flaherty, but director Carroll Ballard comes out of it very well. His movie has the true Flaherty flavor. There is a genuine sense of natural wonder, an imposing vision of the relation between Man and Nature, and a resolution to eschew montage fakery and go for documentary truth. It rejects the contrivance of some of the Disney nature films and relies more on cool observation.

Apart from some rather obvious injections of excitement toward the end – a caribou stampede which traps the naked hero, and the duplicities of the bush pilot and his friend – the movie is virtually plotless. As in Ballard's previous film *The Black Stallion* it compels your attention not through its story but through the vividness of its imagery. Ballard is assisted by a wide range of technical excellence. Mark Isham's score is spare and spooky. The narration is effectively concise, co-written by Eugene Corr who was soon to make an impressive feature-film directing debut with *Desert Bloom* (1985). The Oscar-nominated sound effects are the responsibility of Alan Splet whose talents have contributed so much to the weird atmosphere of the films of David Lynch, such as *Eraserhead* (1976), *The Elephant Man* (1980) and *Blue Velvet* (1986). It is clear from this list of personnel that the movie is aiming for a new style of documentary Disney, with elements of the old tradition but with a tone and style that is now quirky as well as sentimental, edgy as well as emotional. Charles Martin Smith's leading performance is adroitly eccentric and Hiro Narito's photography is superb.

The movie was shot in extraordinarily difficult conditions in Canada's Yukon territory and in Nome, Alaska. Although principal photography was finished in 1980, the film was not ready for release until 1983, which gives some idea of the care Ballard took with the editing and the extent of his perfectionism. There was some critical disagreement over whether the film had entirely solved the tension between narrative and documentary, and the audiences were modest rather than huge, yet the film inspired respect and over the years its reputation has continued to grow. And just as John Ford began to revise his presentation of the Indian in his westerns in his final years, so it is that on the fiftieth anniversary of *Three Little Pigs*, the Disney team has at last made a major movie that is sympathetic in its portrayal of wolves.

BELOW LEFT: Two Eskimo friends for Tyler: Mike (Samson Jorah) and Ootek (Zachary Ittimangnaq). From *Never Cry Wolf*.

RIGHT: Solitary contemplation: Tyler entertains himself amid the awesome scenery.

BELOW: Tyler threatens to open fire on the pilot, who wants the wolves to be killed for their skins.

Something Wicked This Way Comes

1983

Something Wicked This Way Comes is not an obvious contender for inclusion in a survey of the best of Disney. It had a troubled post-production period and was no more successful than the studio's previous horror movie, *The Watcher in the Woods*, in coming up with a satisfactory ending. Indeed, it was to end up as one of the company's biggest box-office flops. Nevertheless it remains one of the most stylish horror films of the decade so far.

The film is based on Ray Bradbury's acclaimed novel about the effect on a small town in Illinois of the visit of a sinister carnival. The novel had once been announced as a future film project for Sam Peckinpah, so there were some raised eyebrows when the Disney organization took it on. However, one should remember that Ray Bradbury was an enormous admirer of Walt Disney, and the novel has many characteristics of the dark fairy tales at which Disney excelled. There is a wicked witch, as well as magic mirrors that recall *Snow White* and a cruel carnival rather as in *Dumbo*. The movie's theme of an innocent with an ineffectual father thrown into a world of monsters and malevolence is strikingly similar to the story of *Pinocchio*. The Studio probably thought it would be reviving that Disney tradition

where a *frisson* of fright accompanies the flight of fantasy.

There was more surprise when the creative personnel were announced. The English filmmaker Jack Clayton was assigned to direct and was allowed to choose many of his own technical team, notably the production designer Richard MacDonald. In his book on Disney, Richard Schickel has described Clayton as the 'kind of reliable second-rater that was comforting to a cautious studio management.' This is unfair to the management and to the director. In fact it was an intelligent and imaginative choice. Clayton had made one of the most eerie and elegant horror films in the history of the cinema, *The Innocents* (1961). Bradbury's story is seen mostly through the eyes of two young boys, and Clayton had already proved himself a superb director of children. His films revealed a recurrent fascination with the theme of loss of innocence, which is at the heart of *Something Wicked*. Although his 1974 movie of *The Great Gatsby* had been torn to shreds by the critics, Clayton had, on the basis of the movie, been hailed as an 'artist' by no less an artistic celebrity than Tennessee Williams (who thought the film even surpassed Fitzgerald's novel) and certainly showed he had a distinctive way of handling an American subject.

In many ways Clayton's direction of *Something Wicked* lives up to his promise. Some of the imagery is quite unforgettable. A fabulous opening shot of a train steaming forward like a black monster announces the approach of the carnival. A ring glitters tantalizingly in a window, enticing susceptible townspeople to enter, fulfill their deepest dreams and then confront their worst nightmares. A merry-go-round goes wrong. The two young boys, who have seen something they should not, dream the same terrifying dream about tarantulas invading their bedroom – as blunt in conception as the rats in *Nineteen-Eighty-Four* perhaps, but still the creepiest scene in a Disney movie for forty years. Quizzing Halloway (Jason Robards) about the whereabouts of his son Will (Vidal Peterson), the evil Mr Dark (Jonathan Pryce) clenches his hand; the blood that leaks forth drops on the face of Will who is hiding in terror under a grating below. Now hiding in the library from Mr Dark, the children peer out anxiously from between the shelves, unaware that two disembodied, black-gloved hands are rising like the tentacles of an octopus behind them.

'I think the message in the film is pretty much the same as in every Disney film,' said Jason Robards during the shooting of the movie. 'We're not making *La Dolce Vita* here.' Well, yes and no. Certainly evil is defeated; the father redeems himself in the eyes of his son by coming to his rescue; the ending is as triumphant in content as it is tentative in tone and execution. Yet the overall atmosphere of the movie remains dark and oppressive. It deals obsessively with devils and death. It turns the American Dream, and the American obsession with youth and fear of ageing, into nightmarish ogres of the imagination. Even the carnival itself seems a subversive symbol. It is Disneyland as seen from the dark side of the moon.

Given the film's mature and disillusioned exploration of what Bradbury's screenplay eloquently calls 'the fearful needs of the human heart' it is perhaps not surprising that *Something Wicked* intimidated audiences more than entranced them. Adults might find Jonathan Pryce's Mr Dark and Pam Grier's Dust Witch a little too disturbingly seductive, and Jason Robards' anguished portrayal of a lifetime of regret a little too painful. Children, on the other hand, would be scared out of their wits by the tarantula scene and the hunt in the library. An uplifting ending might have transcended the terror but, because it does not come off, one is left shaken rather than stirred. Nevertheless, there is some marvelous cinema here. If it is doubtful whether the millions who saw *The Love Bug* can remember anything about it, the handful who saw *Something Wicked This Way Comes* will not have forgotten the experience. Like Charles Laughton's chilling evocation of childhood terror, *The Night of the Hunter* (1955), it changes the quality of your nightmares.

ABOVE LEFT: Mr Dark (Jonathan Pryce) leads a sinister parade through the town in *Something Wicked This Way Comes*.

RIGHT: Hiding from the terrifying Mr Dark, Will (Vidal Peterson, left) notices a spot of blood that has dropped through the grating onto his face. His friend Jim Nightshade (Shawn Carson, right) looks up anxiously.

LEFT: Jonathan Pryce plays Mr Dark, the sinister leader of the carnival.

Mickey's Christmas Carol
1983

According to the critic Gilbert Adair, 'For anyone over thirty-five, this little jewel of a film is truly the Ghost of Christmas Past.' It was a view echoed by many veteran film critics who had come of age during the vintage days of Disney. *Mickey's Christmas Carol* resurrected some of Disney's best-loved characters (it was Mickey Mouse's first film since 1953, a retirement longer than Cagney's). It was also a return to the standards of the classic shorts of the 1930s and was deservedly nominated for an Oscar.

The idea of transporting Disney characters into the world of Dickens had originated in 1974 with the release by Disneyland Records of an album entitled 'Mickey's Christmas Carol.' This in turn had been inspired by a 1967 animation short, *Scrooge McDuck and Money*. The combination of Disney and Charles Dickens might seem peculiar, but they do share a lot of narrative characteristics – a love of sentiment and suspense, humor and horror. Also, as noted earlier, Walt Disney always had a particular affinity for anything to do with Victorian England, so the choice of material is quite appropriate. And of all Dickens's work *A Christmas Carol* is most like a miracle play – the element of the miraculous has always featured prominently in Disney's work.

The first delight of the film is simply one of recognition –

Mickey Mouse as Bob Cratchit, Scrooge's employee, Minnie Mouse as Mrs Cratchit, Donald Duck as Scrooge's nephew, Goofy as Marley's Ghost and Jiminy Cricket as the Ghost of Christmas Past. The Disney characters are cleverly blended with those of Dickens, without any attempt at precise duplication but with sufficient kinship among one another to make the exercise rewarding. As in *Pinocchio* and as is appropriate for his new role as the Ghost of Christmas Past, Jiminy Cricket still represents the voice of conscience; and, as is appropriate for both Cratchit and his own screen persona, Mickey is still the pleasant little guy clinging to his dignity in spite of adverse circumstances.

Elsewhere the references are a bit more obscure and esoteric. The two charity collectors who fail to move Scrooge are Ratty and Moley from *Ichabod and Mr Toad* while the Ghost of Christmas Present is Willie the Giant from *Fun and Fancy Free*. The Ghost of Christmas Future is drawn like a cross between Peg Leg Pete and Chernabog in *Fantasia*. Also glimpsed at Scrooge's childhood party are those two lively chipmunks, Chip 'n' Dale, and Donald Duck's horse is Cyril Proudbottom who appears in *The Adventures of Ichabod and Mr Toad*.

Disney seems most like Dickens in the moments of grotesquerie around Scrooge's lonely grave and his frightening descent toward the flames of hellfire. The Dickensian narrative is transformed into the Disney style most noticeably when Jacob Marley becomes a comic figure and Scrooge

BELOW LEFT: The Cratchit family at Christmas: that is, Mickey Mouse, Minnie and their 'children.' From *Mickey's Christmas Carol*.

RIGHT: Donald Duck makes his usual boisterous appearance as Scrooge's nephew.

BELOW: Scrooge McDuck, the miserable miser about to discover the milk of human kindness.

discovers the art of flying on his journey back to his past ('What's wrong, Scrooge?' says his escort, 'I thought you enjoyed looking down on the world'). Dickens's characterization always tended to caricature, so his representation in cartoon form does less violence to his style than it would other writers. His stories also always lent themselves to vivid illustration, and this is another aspect of his style on which Disney's animators have been able to capitalize.

Burny Mattinson supervised the direction and the film cost $3 million, a lot of money for a short. (However, as it was the supporting feature for the successful reissue of *The Jungle Book*, it recouped its cost.) The money was clearly well spent because there is some fine animation in the best Disney tradition – the slapstick comedy of Goofy's Marley or the moments that move between niceness and nightmare. Perhaps most distinctive is the translucent tear that Mickey sheds by Tiny Tim's gravestone – a reference both to the largeness of Dickensian sentiment and the purity of Disneyesque emotion. It is a poignant memory of the style that brought us the wax melting from the candle in imitation of the dwarfs' grief when they think Snow White is dead, or the crystalline raindrops in *Bambi*.

Perhaps the main appeal of the story for the Disney team was its potential for use as an allegory about Disneyesque entertainment. When Mickey wishes Scrooge a Merry Christmas as he leaves the counting house, the miserable old miser says, 'Never mind the mushy stuff, just go!' How many cynics have approached a new Disney movie with much the same sentiments and yet found themselves transported by the film's emotional world? In Dickens's tale Scrooge is transformed by a benevolence and love that seems part of the air around him – only perversity has prevented him from breathing it in for so long. In *Mickey's Christmas Carol* the Disney animators have boldly gone for a very similar atmosphere, and if one is to judge by the reaction of press and public alike to the film they succeeded triumphantly.

RIGHT: The faithful Bob Cratchit (Mickey Mouse) at work as Scrooge's employee. From *Mickey's Christmas Carol*.

FAR RIGHT: The Cratchits are overwhelmed by the Christmas generosity of Mr Scrooge.

BELOW RIGHT: Scrooge catches Cratchit putting an extra lump of coal on the fire.

LEFT: Still deserving of an award for conscience: Jiminy Cricket appears as the ghost of Christmas Past.

BELOW: Goofy, as the ghost of Bob Marley, advises Scrooge to mend his ways: as usual, Goofy has discovered that he did it all wrong.

The Journey of Natty Gann
1985

Appearing unheralded toward the end of 1985, *The Journey of Natty Gann* is an unexpected gem of family entertainment and a tour de force of fine moviemaking. It is based on a superb original screenplay by Jeanne Rosenberg who was one of the co-writers of *The Black Stallion*, and is directed with sensitivity and imagination by Jeremy Kagan whose erratic film career to date has included offbeat movies like *The Big Fix* (1978) and *The Chosen* (1981) as well as chores like *The Sting 2* (1983). The movie works because it has been fashioned by people who seem to respect the Disney tradition but who are also not afraid to try something which is a little off the beaten track.

The setting is Chicago in 1935, a time of low wages and high unemployment. A union activist, Sol Gann (Ray Wise), is offered a job as a lumberjack in Washington State, clearly to get him off the backs of the management. 'You have no choice, it's a job,' a friend tells him, but he has to depart before having the chance to say goodbye to his twelve-year-old daughter, Natty (Meredith Salenger). Entrusted by Sol with the care of Natty, the landlady Connie (Lainie Kazan) rapidly becomes exasperated, particularly when the police bring Natty home after she has been throwing stones at them for evicting her friends. When Connie plans to hand her over to the authorities, Natty escapes and resolves to find her father by 'riding the rails' with the other hobos. Many adventures will occur during the journey – she will be put away in an institution for delinquents and will also have to resist the advances of a lecherous driver. She will be helped by a young hobo, Harry (John Cusack). Most importantly she will be befriended by a wolf, whom she has helped escape from a group of drunken oafs. After a few edgy encounters with Natty, the wolf will accompany her on her journey until both find what they are looking for.

Early in the film there is a moment when Natty and her friends are seen spying into a movie theater which is showing a Mickey Mouse cartoon. It is a reference to classic Disney, and the movie plays a lot of canny games with conventions we recognize from Disney's films. As an inveterate train-lover, Walt would have adored the whole business connected with 'riding the rails' – *Natty Gann* is the best train movie from Disney since *The Great Locomotive Chase*. The plot has similarities to *The Incredible Journey* (1963) and even *In Search of the Castaways*, and a character like the landlady, Connie, is an ingenious variation on the familiar Disney ogre of the wicked stepmother. When Natty sees the wolf being carried away in a van seemingly to its death, one thinks of the similar scene with the dog-catcher's van in *Lady and the Tramp*. When Natty deliberately distracts the aim of an adult to stop him shooting an animal, one recalls a similar moment in *The Sword in the Stone*. All the Disney ingredients are there – suspense and excitement, emotional warmth, the love and yet pain of separation between parent and child, children and animals. The structure is classic Disney, where a sprinkling of diverting incident cannot disperse an overhanging atmosphere of anxiety until a cathartic climax. William Dean Howells once said that the stories Americans like best are 'tragedies with a happy ending.' It is a good description of much of Disney, and of *Natty Gann*.

The darker, more adult side of *Natty Gann* has something of the quality that one remembers from the very best Disney – a quality that can intrigue adults as well as it can enthrall children. *Natty Gann* suddenly reminds one of how often Disney's films in the 1930s were compared with those of Chaplin for it has much in common with Chaplin's *Modern Times* (1936). Like Chaplin it recreates the harshness of the time – the desolation of unemployment, the occasional brutality of the police. Harry's father, like the heroine's father in *Modern Times*, is a victim of the violence of the time – crushed in a stampede for a job. Like Chaplin's thieves in *Modern Times* also, no condemnation is invited of the 'family' Natty encounters of petty criminals trying to survive in a hideous situation against a hostile society. When a hobo camp is set on fire by vigilantes Harry bitterly identifies them for Natty as 'the Main Streeters – good, law-abiding citizens. They don't like the way we live.' For a Disney movie this is hard-hitting stuff and Paul Sylbert's production design makes one feel the texture of the times.

Against this bleak social background in which the adult world is seen as hostile and threatening, the movie sets up a bond of friendship between girl and wolf that moves the film onto a more poetic plane. Yet the bond is not sentimentally contrived, but very intelligently set up. Natty helps the wolf

RIGHT: A courageous young girl (Meredith Salenger), a young drifter (John Cusack) and an untamed wolf find themselves cast together in *The Journey of Natty Gann*.

in that first ferocious fight because, like her, it is struggling for survival in a disgusting, dog-eat-dog man's world. Also it is some time before Natty conquers her fear of the animal – it often strides suddenly toward her out of the darkness, like a symbol of Natty's suppressed terror moving frighteningly into the forefront of her consciousness. The stages by which Natty and the wolf come to trust each other are very sensitively prepared, particularly in the scenes in the forest, magically scored by James Horner in thematic fragments evocative of Mahler's *Song of the Earth*.

One of the movie's boldest decisions was probably to make the main character a girl, and not a boy. Her resourcefulness and courage make a refreshing change from the passivity of most modern screen heroines, and Jeanne Rosenberg handles the woman's theme in the film extremely well. Meredith Salenger's performance could not be bettered, and her fondness for Harry (another first-rate performance from John Cusack) is very gently conveyed in a restrained farewell scene at a bus station and in a delightful moment of bashfulness when Natty almost signs off her letter to him with the word 'Love,' but then, overcome by shyness, she blushes, laughs, and just puts her name instead.

The filming is often spectacular, particularly those shots of Gann swaying on the topmost parts of a tree, fatalistically pursuing the most dangerous work now that he believes his beloved Natty has been killed. Dick Bush's photography often takes one's breath away in its responsiveness to landscape, though the film's most moving piece of photography is the glow that irradiates Natty's tent after she has bidden a heartbroken goodbye to the wolf. Initially contrasting with her mood of desolation, the warm light actually anticipates the golden news to come of the discovery of her father.

'That's a nice dog,' an impoverished tramp says to Natty, which precipitates a growl and Natty's reply, 'He's a wolf.' The skill of this moment is that the wolf growls not on the word 'nice' (which would be straightforward irony) but on the word 'dog' (which is a real insult and to which the wolf takes haughty exception – like calling a 'limousine' a 'cab'). Even the wolf has exquisite comic timing in *Natty Gann*. This is one of those rare Disney movies that slipped out rather quietly but has gradually acquired a following. But it deserves not just a cult reputation but a recognition as something quite exceptional – the best live-action film ever to come out of Disney studios.

CHAPTER FIVE

Dream Come True

The Creation of Disneyland

Whether Walt Disney can be regarded as an artist is open to debate (he professed not to care), but one thing is certain: he raised business acumen to the level of artistic inspiration, and in a business like the cinema which is an industry *and* an art this is a priceless asset. No one grasped more quickly the opportunities that sound, color, multiplane camera, feature-length, stereo and CinemaScope offered to the animated film: in every instance, he was in there first. No one perceived better than he the merchandising possibilities of film from spin-off sales of toys, books, records, and so on. Nobody in the film business adjusted more quickly to the challenge of television and utilized it better to his advantage. Disney had infinite patience but he was courageous more than cautious and, if he was never an intellectual, his intuition was so sound that intellect was hardly ever missed.

If his movies contain many wonders, they also, in a few odd instances, leave one wondering. Is it not strange that the most fearsome villains in Disney, like those in *Snow White*, *Cinderella*, *101 Dalmatians*, even *The Sword in the Stone*, are women? The male rogues, like Captain Hook, tend to have redeeming features, but the villainesses are mainly evil through and through. We await an explanation for this mystery from the feminist film fraternity: there was nothing in Disney's life that would explain it.

Also, for a man so closely identified with the purest Americana (some call it 'Americorna'), is it not odd that so much of Disney's inspiration comes from British sources? Among the British authors he has adapted are Robert Louis Stevenson, A A Milne, Sir Walter Scott, J M Barrie, Kenneth Grahame, Lewis Carroll, Rudyard Kipling and (if one includes those films that continue the Disney tradition after his death), Charles Dickens and Arthur Conan Doyle. This is not to mention those other works actually set in England, like *101 Dalmatians* and *Mary Poppins*, and those that deal with English history and legend, like *The Sword in the Stone* and *Robin Hood*. One could even extend this further and note that two of the Oscar-winning performances he drew from humans were also from English actors – Hayley Mills in *Pollyanna* and Julie Andrews in *Mary Poppins*. We know there was a time when simple economics explained the amount of English material in Disney's production line-up, but it does not explain the attraction throughout his career of English material over corresponding American classics, which seem hardly to have inspired him at all. Did he believe that Americans possessed no adequate legends of their own, or that John Ford had already done them? Did he want to Americanize European culture? It is indeed a curious matter, and there is still a good deal to be pondered about British influences on Disney.

What about Disney's own influence on the cinema? Quotations from, and references to Disney in the work of other filmmakers have been mentioned throughout this book, and there is no more striking example of Disney's influence than the work of Steven Spielberg. Viewed from a Disneyesque perspective *Jaws* looks like a cross between *Peter Pan* and *Three Little Pigs* and could even be subtitled *20,000 Legs Under the Sea*. *E.T.* owes much to *Bambi*; even *The Color Purple* looks like an imaginative Spielberg blend of *Dumbo* and *Song of the South*. Spielberg is Disney's cinematic son. He shares the same instinct for gripping storytelling; the same hotline to an audience's emotions, so that tears and terror can be provoked at will; the same flair for the right music and the dazzling special effect; and a similar cinematic world that countenances no contradictions and admits no ambiguities. Spielberg movies like *Raiders of the Lost Ark* (1981) and his production, *The Goonies* (1985), function less like logical narratives than like a two-hour ride on a Disneyland rollercoaster. It seems inevitable that Spielberg would move into the field of the animated feature, and with Disney-deserter Don Bluth as director, produce *An American Tail* (1986). One need hardly add that the hero is a mouse.

Disney's fame and influence have come mainly through the movies, but perhaps his proudest monument is the Disneyland theme park, an idea that burgeoned in Disney's mind over a period of twenty years. It finally opened at its site at Anaheim near Los Angeles on his thirtieth wedding anniversary, on 17 July 1955. In the words of the original folder written by Bill Walsh and approved by Disney, its aim was 'to be a place for people to find happiness and knowledge'; to be 'based upon and dedicated to the ideals, the dreams and hard facts that have created America'; and to be 'filled with the accomplishments, the joys and hopes of the world we live in.' One might add that its other aims, fully achieved, were to be as efficient as the Disney studios and as popular as the Disney movies. The main areas are Tomorrowland which celebrates Disney's fascination with technological advances, Fantasyland which evokes the world of his animated cartoons, Adventureland which aims for the excitement of the nature films, and Frontierland which is a tribute to the old American pioneer whose spirit Disney might be said to have inherited. An equally awesome theme park, Walt Disney World resort was opened in Florida in 1971, followed by the Tokyo Disneyland park in 1983.

Art Babbitt, who had no reason to love Disney, said recently, 'Animation would never have reached the peak it did if it hadn't been for Disney.' He was an entrepreneur tireless in his quest for excellence, and matchless, in Ward Kimball's words, 'at getting things out of you that you didn't know you'd got.' As for the enduring appeal of his work, one is reminded of G K Chesterton's comment on the phenomenal popularity of Dickens – it was not simply that he knew what the public wanted, it was that he *wanted* what the public wanted. This was the reason Disney could sell his product with complete conviction and with perfect sincerity. And why should he not believe in fairy tales? With the creation of Disneyland, he had succeeded in building his own Utopia. How could his work come over as anything other than an unequivocal affirmation of the American Dream? After all, he had dreamed it himself – and it all came true.

ABOVE: Sleeping Beauty Castle, a favorite attraction at Disneyland.

RIGHT: The Walt Disney World skyline at night.

LEFT: Walt Disney at his beloved Disneyland in 1955 – a dream come true.

RIGHT: Disneyland – the world-famous theme park opened on 17 July 1955.

ABOVE: Walt Disney World opened on 1 October 1971.

Index

Acknowledgments

We would like to thank The Walt Disney Company for permission to reproduce the illustrations in this book. In addition our thanks go to David Eldred, the designer; Wendy Sacks, the editor; Jean Chiaramonte Martin, the picture researcher; and Diana LeCore, the indexer.